MAIN LENDING   **3 WEEK LOAN**   DCU LIBRARY

Fines are charged **PER DAY** if this item is overdue.
Check at www.dcu.ie/~library or telephone (01) 700 5183 for fine rates and
renewal regulations for this item type.
Item is subject to recall.
Remember to use the Book Bin when the library is closed.
The item is due for return on or before the latest date shown below.

	1 3 JUL 2007	
17 OCT 2006	2 1 MAY 2008	
1 4 DEC 2006	1 1 JUN 2008	
2 6 MAY 2007		
0 8 JUN 2007		
2 9 APR 2008		

Broadcasting in a Divided Community

Seventy Years of the BBC in Northern Ireland

Edited by Martin McLoone

Institute of Irish Studies
The Queen's University of Belfast

Published 1996
The Institute of Irish Studies
The Queen's University of Belfast

Grateful acknowledgement for financial assistance is made to the
Cultural Traditions Group of the Community Relations Council,
which aims to encourage acceptance and understanding of cultural
diversity, and to the University of Ulster.

ISBN 085389 620 8

Printed by W. & G. Baird Ltd., Antrim

CONTENTS

INTRODUCTION

Martin McLoone

The BBC (then the British Broadcasting Company) inaugurated its service from Belfast on 15 September 1924. During 1994, the BBC celebrated its seventieth anniversary with a series of special programming culled from its extensive radio and television archives. A broadcasting exhibition toured Northern Ireland and a number of public meetings were called involving top BBC executives. This year of celebration ended with a one-day symposium held under the auspices of the School of Media and Performing Arts at the University of Ulster at Coleraine, at which many of the papers included in the present volume were first read. A number of other chapters were specially commissioned for the volume. The original symposium was designed to bring together in a public forum, and in constructive dialogue, the broadcasters and those media academics who have an interest in the history, development and future direction of public service broadcasting. The aim of this collection is to bring to a wider public the results of these deliberations.

This type of dialogue is important because the recent history of broadcasting in the UK (and Ireland) has shown that the continued existence of public service broadcasting cannot be taken for granted. In the government Green Paper on the future of the BBC, published in 1993, one of the key questions posed was whether or not public service broadcasting was 'an idea which has had its day'.[1] The BBC itself responded vigorously to the Green Paper in its own policy document for the future, strategically called *Extending Choice*, and by and large, the government's final proposals, confirming the BBC's charter until the year 2006, has accepted the perspective outlined in this document.[2]

In retrospect, though, it now looks like a close run thing. There is a general feeling that had Mrs. Thatcher survived in government for a little longer, then the original Green Paper would have been much more abrasive, not only about the BBC, but also about the very concept of public service broadcasting itself. There are many factors which have combined in recent years to bring about this crisis for a concept that had once seemed beyond questioning. On one hand, technological changes in broadcasting itself has proliferated the number of channels and delivery systems available to a public which has shown itself willing to pay. (After a slow start, both satellite and cable have gained a significant presence in the broadcasting market in the UK.) There was also a growing feeling that as the television audience diversified and the BBC share began to decline, then it was increasingly more difficult (and politically less expedient) to justify a licence fee which supported the BBC only. The major problem, though, was ideological and political. In the 1980s, the Thatcher government was fundamentally hostile to the post-war consensus and sceptical of its public service achievements and began to look for ways of privatising public utilities. The BBC was an obvious target, especially for a government which also felt that market forces could be relied upon to deliver a media system more politically supportive of its underlying ideology than that which the public service requirements and traditions of the BBC could offer.

In these circumstances, the very idea of public service broadcasting needs to be openly interrogated and publicly debated. It is not just that the concept needs to be defended against hostile opponents, be these multi-national media conglomerates, national commercial interests or a hostile government. It is also the case that the supporters of public service broadcasting must ensure that the concept is defined and re-defined, its aims and objectives continuously updated and made relevant to a changing social and economic environment. The marking and celebrating of the BBC's anniversary, then, has provided an opportunity to do just this and has, therefore, been as much concerned with the future as it has been about the past. This is also the case with the essays in the present volume.

In the first contribution, Paddy Scannell looks back to the formative years of the BBC in the early 1920s and sketches out the development of its regional policy, the context within which the opening of the Belfast office in 1924 took place. Scannell argues that in the first few years of its development, the BBC allowed a truly local service to emerge but that from 1927 on, when the Company was restructured as a public body under Royal Charter, a process of centralisation resulted in a service that became increasingly more metropolitan-centred. He argues that the future of public service broadcasting depends on re-discovering the closeness with regional and local audiences which was lost in the centralising process of the late 1920s and 1930s. It took many years for this process to be challenged and reversed and in his chapter, Des Cranston traces the slow but inevitable re-assertion of regional and local identity in the development of radio in Northern Ireland. He also argues for the importance of radio as a medium, not only of entertainment and information but as a channel for harnessing and representing a sense of local identity. The success of Radio Ulster and Radio Foyle demonstrates just how far the metropolitan bias of the BBC has been changed, at least on radio.

In the first of two contributions to the book, Martin McLoone considers and contrasts the development of the BBC in Belfast with Radio Éireann in Dublin and argues that, because of the prevailing orthodoxy in both states at the time, radio became an important force in consolidating a partitionist mentality North and South, this despite its capacity to cross borders and the hopes expressed at the outset of the broadcasting era about its ability to bring people closer together. He also discusses the way in which the demand for local autonomy and a greater level of indigenous programming was linked to the perception that broadcasting would play a crucial role in both promoting and maintaining a sense of cultural identity. The versions of both 'Britishness' and 'Irishness' which were increasingly promoted in both states at the time were particularly narrow and exclusive ones. The irony is that, in a later phase, after the coming of television, broadcasting was to play an equally crucial role in throwing the fixed certainties of the past into crisis.

The history of public service broadcasting and the BBC in Northern Ireland was always a fraught and contradictory one. If the BBC, as Scannell makes clear, was an important agency for promoting and sustaining a consensus notion of 'Britishness' within the UK as a whole, this role was considerably compromised in the divided community of the North, where notions of 'Britishness' were at the centre of controversy and dispute. Many of the contributors pick up on this central dilemma. James Hawthorne, who was later to become BBC NI Controller, describes the quite difficult development of an Irish history series for the schools radio service in the early 1960s. This was always likely to be

a controversial development, given the disputed nature of Irish
history in the first place but, as he describes it, the new service also
had to face considerable opposition from within the BBC in
Belfast as well as from the ruling Unionist establishment of the
day. This schools service, in a careful, balanced and objective manner, introduced into local broadcasting, almost for the first time,
an acknowledgement of the fact that there existed a tradition
which fundamentally opposed the prevailing orthodoxy about
'Britishness'. In doing so, it also broached for the first time, albeit
indirectly, the basic lack of consensus in Northern Ireland and
while it was hoped at the time that such an open engagement with
controversy would facilitate dialogue and a greater understanding
between the opposing traditions, the period during which the programmes were made and broadcast was to show that the resentment and fear had probably gestated too long for broadcasting to
do any more than chart the coming crisis.

The reluctance to deal with Irish history was symptomatic of the
more general problem of a conflict over identity and this is
addressed by the current Controller of BBC NI, Pat Loughrey, who
looks back at both the shortcomings and the achievements of the
past in regard to the BBC's cultural remit. In doing so, he also
looks to the future and offers a view of how this remit will be
addressed in the period of the new Royal Charter. With its
medium term future secure, the BBC in Northern Ireland has
now, quite rightly, begun to look at what its role should be in the
post-ceasefire cultural climate and Pat Loughrey's assessment of
both the strengths and the weaknesses of the past is an important
step in mapping out the future.

The approaching storms which could at least be sensed in the
relative calm of the 1960s, burst into public view on television on
5 October, 1968 and for the next twenty-five years, the BBC
(together with other broadcasters) was never far from controversy
in regard to the manner in which it attempted to cover the deep-
ening crisis. Martin McLoone looks at some drama productions
over these years and argues that while there has undoubtedly been
some significant achievements, these tended to be in rather
uncontroversial areas politically. Even the best drama tended to
ignore the politics of the situation in favour of human interest sto-
rylines and in the process, often despite their best intentions,
offered rather banal or stereotyped analysis of the politics that
underpinned the situation. Only rarely did television drama try to

go beyond the limitations increasingly imposed on journalists, and even then, these were largely in the field of documentary drama, which invariably worked from a news and current affairs agenda anyway.

A number of chapters address this question of news and current affairs coverage. Keith Kyle describes his experiences working for the BBC in the early years of the troubles and he outlines the pressures that journalists had to contend with, both from the attentions of government and an increasingly worried broadcasting institution and from their own awareness of how news reporting could actually fan the flames of violence. He describes a number of cases in which this pressure operated and charts some instances of the creeping self-imposed and externally-imposed forms of censorship that constantly hindered the journalist from pursuing stories in investigative detail. Keith Baker gives an institutional context to these issues, gleaned from his experiences over many years of working in the BBC newsroom. David Butler outlines the problems which face the media academic in trying to analyse and make sense of these institutional experiences and points out that the basic problem facing the BBC in particular, was that it was trying to perform a basically consensual role in a deeply divided community where no consensus existed.

The final three chapters address more directly aspects of the BBC's future. Liz Fawcett was a journalist in the BBC in Belfast for a number of years and researched attitudes among women journalists there about their working environment in a traditionally male profession. Interestingly enough, she hears from a number of journalists who felt that over the years, the institutional practices of the profession discouraged women from seeking, or expecting, promotion to senior positions. In recent years, the BBC has introduced a series of measures to encourage women to stay in the profession and Liz Fawcett also considers how effective these are likely to be. (Since these chapters are designed to allow the reader to experience a dialogue between the broadcasters and the academics, it is only fair to point out that the success of the BBC in attracting and holding on to well-qualified women is greater than the situation which pertains in the universities. According to a recent article in the *Times Higher Educational Supplement*, despite the fact that women now account for about fifty per cent of undergraduates at most universities, only five per cent of professorships in the UK, and only sixteen per cent in the US, are held by women.[3] The fact that there is only one women contributor to this volume is indicative, perhaps, of the need for the universities, more so than the broadcasters, to re-think their recruitment and promotion strategies.)

The present national Governor for Northern Ireland is Sir Ken Bloomfield and in his chapter, he considers in detail the development of the Governors' role (which he sees as a form of 'trusteeship' of the public service requirements of the BBC) and is careful to try and delineate the point at which the roles and responsibilities of the Board of Governors and the Management diverge. Finally, the current Deputy Director General of the BBC, Bob Phillis, outlines the future direction of the BBC as it moves towards the new millennium and explains in broad terms what the implications are of the new Charter arrangements as set out in the White Paper.

This volume, then, marks the seventieth anniversary of the BBC in Northern Ireland and looks at aspects of its past and future direction. All the contributors are united in their commitment to the principle of public service broadcasting and are conscious of the role that the BBC in Northern Ireland has played, and will continue to play, in mediating the politics and culture of a deeply divided community. By understanding both the achievements and shortcomings of the past, it is hoped that the BBC, secure in its public service role, will play a significant part in the development of the cultural life of Northern Ireland as it grapples with the implications of the ceasefires and the policy of 'parity-of-esteem' for the conflicting senses of identity which lie at the heart of recent problems.

These essays do not, however, amount to a comprehensive historical analysis of the BBC over the last seventy years. The best historical survey is still Rex Cathcart's 'official' history, *The Most Contrary Region*,[4] and it is testament to the enduring value of this work that so many of the contributors draw on it for historical detail. During the year that marked the BBC's anniversary, Professor Cathcart died and the broadcasting and academic communities of Northern Ireland were united in their sorrow at the passing of a man who had done so much for both the development of broadcasting in Northern Ireland and for the academic study of broadcasting's history and social impact. It is fitting that he should be remembered in a volume of essays devoted to the institution whose history he so assiduously chronicled.

NOTES

1. Department of National Heritage, *The Future of the BBC: A Consultation Document*, Cm. 2098, (London, HMSO, 1992).
2. BBC, *Extending Choice: The BBC's Role in the New Broadcasting Age* (London: BBC, 1992) and Department of National Heritage, *The Future of the BBC: Serving the Nation, Competing World-Wide*, Cm. 2621 (London: HMSO, 1994).
3. Helena Kennedy, 'Prisoners of gender', *Times Higher Educational Supplement*, 3 November, 1995, pp.15-16.
4. Rex Cathcart, *The Most Contrary Region: The BBC in Northern Ireland 1924-84* (Belfast: The Blackstaff Press, 1984).

THE ORIGINS OF BBC REGIONAL POLICY *

Paddy Scannell

Introduction

In its formative period, from its beginnings in the early 20s to the outbreak of war in 1939, the BBC defined its programme services for its audiences in three different ways, as local, national and regional. In the very early years from 1923 to the end of 1926, broadcasting developed on a local basis. But by 1925 there were already plans afoot to change this and to create a centralised national service with an alternative regional choice. Three different models, then, of the relationship between broadcasting and its audiences, each with very different social and cultural implications, were figured in the BBC's development from the very beginning. The hierarchy of values that accumulated around these three possible variants within a public service model in the early years have left their traces on the BBC right through to the present. Thus the strategic and organisational assumptions underpinning *Extending Choice* in the 90s have their roots in key organisational decisions and cultural assumptions some seventy years earlier. Today the BBC declares its intention to 'make network radio and television programmes in designated regional production centres – in Belfast, Birmingham, Bristol, Cardiff, Glasgow and Manchester'.[1] The rationale for these places as designated 'regional' production centres was worked out in the 20s.

Local Broadcasting: 1923-6

When the British Broadcasting Company began transmitting programmes in late 1922, it did so from three radio stations in Manchester, Birmingham and London. These stations were inherited from three of the leading radio-electronics companies with major interests in the newly founded BBC – respectively, Metro Vickers, Western Electric and Marconi. The immediate and pressing task of the infant BBC was to make its service, within economic and technical constraints, as widely available as possible. The initial plan was to establish radio stations in the major centres of population throughout Britain, thereby enticing the majority of the population to experiment with the newfangled pleasure of 'listening-in'. Accordingly it was intended to establish, alongside the original three, further stations in Newcastle, Cardiff, Glasgow, Aberdeen, Bournemouth and Belfast. These nine 'main stations', as they were called, each began operating independently, producing about six hours of their own programme material each day. Their effective range of reception was twenty miles at most and many neighbouring urban centres could not get adequate reception from them. And so, in the next few years, a number of smaller 'relay stations' were set up to increase coverage. Sheffield was the first, in 1924, quickly followed by Plymouth, Edinburgh, Liverpool, Leeds-Bradford (a unique 'twin station'), Hull, Nottingham, Dundee, Stoke-on-Trent and Swansea. It was originally intended that these stations should simply relay programme material from the nearest main station, but that was not how things developed.

The problem arose, at the start, with Sheffield where there was considerable civic interest in radio and its possibilities.[2] The original plan was to link it to Manchester but there were loudly voiced local objections to this.[3] Why should Sheffield not make its own programmes? Why should a Yorkshire city have to listen to programmes from Lancashire? The BBC gave in on both fronts. Sheffield was allowed a tiny staff and a small amount of local programming, and for the rest of the time it transmitted the service of the London station. The same policy was subsequently applied to all the other relay stations, and so from the very start (without any pressure from London) the metropolitan service began to assume a greater importance than all other stations in the system. Reith thought it silly that the places in which radio stations were to be sited should see it as an affront to their dignity to be linked to, say, Birmingham, rather than London. But perhaps what it indicates is a demand for a balance between local broadcasting, on the one hand, and at the same time a link with the centre of national life. Sheffield wanted first and foremost its own programme service and then to be able to pick and choose from the best on offer from London. What it and the other relay stations got, however, was the reverse: a very small amount of locally produced programmes and a very large amount of London's output.

All the stations were linked directly to London, and indirectly to each other, via Post Office land lines and so it was possible for a transmission from any station to be taken by all the others in what was, in effect, a national network. The technique of what were called 'simultaneous broadcasts' (SBs) on which the relay stations depended thus had a wider potential for the pooling of resources throughout the country. In this network, London, from the start, had a key position and while other stations could and did provide SBs, the principle was established in 1923 that two complete evenings a week should be supplied by London to all the other stations. London, it was claimed, could supply not only the networked news bulletins but also outstanding artists, concerts and public events that could not be matched elsewhere.

In a few years' time this would be expanded into a much larger claim for a broadcasting service based in London as the political, social and cultural heart of the nation. But Reith at first envisaged a different kind of development for the infant service, with radio stations eventually grouped according to the regional characteristics of the populations in the areas they covered. Main stations would develop the quality of their services to make them acceptable to neighbouring relay stations thereby weaning them off their dependence on London. London would arrange important cultural and entertainment programmes for SB transmission to the rest of the network on London Special Nights.[4] In this scheme of things, main and local stations would develop into regional networks that expressed the character of places and people in the area served, while being able to tap London for programmes of wider and more general interest. And, to an extent, that is how radio did develop for its first few years.[5]

In all sorts of ways the early BBC stations sought to establish an interactive relationship with their audiences, a relationship in which the broadcasters did not set themselves up as superior to their listeners but treated them as equals and acknowledged that they were accountable to them. The stations tried to become integral parts of the local community, working with the civic authorities, with local cultural organisations, businesses, universities and schools, churches, hospitals and so forth. They were open to their publics. Several graphic accounts survive, for instance, of the Leeds-Bradford station, of the casual visitors who used to 'drop in' and the notices warning them to be silent during live transmissions.[6] The early stations worked as what we might now call community services: that is, they interacted with and became part of their local culture. The mere fact that early radio depended in large measure on local resources for its programmes, compelled the broadcasters to get out into the community, to work with local people, in order to produce a local service. The real and valuable qualities of this kind of service were not adequately recognised at the time, and were lost for many years. Broadcasting, in its beginnings, was in many ways more genuinely local than BBC local radio is today.

The Regional Scheme: 1925-30

From late 1923 Reith began a concerted policy to exercise greater control over the activities of the stations. In the next couple of years a small management system based at Head Office (that is, London) began to impose a common policy over the whole system. It was one which involved a retreat from the informal, friendly and accessible manner of the local stations into a distant, aloof and formal style of broadcasting. The diversity of the individual stations, and the sometimes heterodox activities of their station directors, was carefully brought to heel. Reith's vision of broadcasting was changing. More and more he thought of the BBC as a national institution providing a national broadcasting service. This was central to the concept of public service which he vigorously and cogently promoted from 1924 onwards, and particularly in evidence to the Crawford Committee (1925) which recommended changing the status of the BBC from a private company serving the interests of the British radio industry to a public corporation under the auspices of the state. The Charter and Licence, which confirmed this transformation in 1926, gave the BBC a remit to develop broadcasting 'as a national service in the public interest'.

Plans to restructure broadcasting had been discussed since early 1925 and as they took shape they were labelled 'The Regional Scheme', with Peter Eckersley (the BBC's Chief Engineer) as its principal architect, though regionalism had precious little to do with it at first. It was clear that broadcasting could not continue to develop along its original lines. The nineteen stations that made up the original network covered, between them, about 80 per cent of the population. It was obviously uneconomic to try and reach the remaining 20 per cent of the population – in remoter areas with sparser, scattered populations – by the incremental addition of more low-power stations with a small reception area. There were obvious economies to be made in programme production by eliminating the duplication of material by the nine main stations. At the same time it was becoming unfeasible to continue with nineteen stations on nineteen different wavelengths. Transmissions from stations in mainland Europe were beginning to interfere with BBC transmissions on similar wavelengths. Cross-border interference required international agreements to establish a common European policy for the allocation of frequencies on a nation-by-nation basis. Peter Eckersley was involved in these developments from the beginning, and was ready to concede that the BBC should lose some frequencies in order to establish a proper regulatory framework for Europe that would avoid the 'chaos of the ether' that was perceived to have happened in the United States. The Geneva Plan of 1926, in which Eckersley played a major role, halved the number of medium wavelengths available to the BBC at that time.

With ten frequencies instead of twenty to play with, Eckersley came up with a plan for their optimum usage. The nub of his scheme was to provide listeners anywhere in Britain with a choice of listening to one or other of two BBC programme services. The underlying rationale for the proposal was that it obviated one of the most obvious criticisms of the BBC's monopoly – namely that it denied listeners freedom of choice. Accordingly Eckersley proposed setting up five high-powered transmission centres each using two different wavelengths to transmit two different programme services. These centres were to be based in 'different Regions of the British Isles so that, in combination, and with their much higher power, the transmitters would spread their dual programme over all the territory to be served'.[7]

The five 'regions' proposed by Eckersley were:

1. London (for the Home Counties).
2. Birmingham (Midlands).
3. Manchester (for the Industrial North).
4. Cardiff (for Wales and the West of England).
5. Glasgow (for Scotland).

By synchronising some wavelengths and transmitting the same (National) programme at each centre some wavelengths could be 'saved' to cover Belfast and the north-east coast from single-wave transmitters. But what should be the principle on which this ser-

vice was based? Speech on one, music on the other was one possibility. 'Universal' and 'specialist' programmes was a distinction put
forward by Eckersley. There was talk of a third 'uplift' channel –
which would be the broadcast equivalent of *The Times* and the
Spectator – but for the time being this Third Programme remained
a mere gleam in the corporate eye. That it should have some
regional basis to it was conceded, but what exactly that meant was
far from clear when, in vague and uncertain terms, the new
arrangements were announced:

> It is in fact impossible to formulate any one principle which will
> be an infallible guide in every case of doubt, but it has been
> found that a useful test to apply is the distinction between items
> which demand concentrated listening and those which repay
> more casual listening.[8]

The Development of the Regional Programme

Thereafter the Regional Scheme unfolded, as Briggs remarks,
with all the inevitability of gradualism. It was the National rather
than the Regional Programme that was set in place first, of course.
This London-based service began in 1930, and the Regional
Programme, spreading throughout Britain in the next decade,
was from the start structured in subordination to the London programme. The key concept that defined the in-house definition
and development of the Regional Scheme was 'centralisation', a
policy that was imposed from the centre on the margins in a strik-
ingly insensitive way. The newly designated regional directors
found their resources severely cut back (especially in the matter of
'regional' orchestras, which were at first reduced to octets!) as
they were told to apply the rule that if London could do it better,
they should not attempt it.

Underlying centralisation was the unquestioned assumption
that metropolitan culture was superior to provincial culture.
London had access, it went without saying, to better quality per-
formers and performances in the arts, music and entertainment.
In political, literary and artistic life it could draw upon the great
and good – politicians, pundits and men of letters – to come to the
microphone and hold forth. In comparison with the riches to be
tapped by the centre, the resources of the provinces seemed sec-
ond-rate. What could the provinces produce that London could
not? They could reflect the life and variety of the areas they cov-

ered. And so, by default, the regions came to excel in programmes that reflected back to their audiences the culture of everyday life in the areas they served. The two kinds of programme-making to take the lead in such developments were outside broadcasts and features (or documentaries as we would call them).

At first though, the effect of the policy of centralisation, and the brusque manner in which it was implemented by departmental heads in London, produced a sense that programme-making in the provinces was 'a weary, flat, stale and unprofitable affair', as Scotland's Regional Director put it. Ted Liveing, the Director of North Region, summed up the general view with admirable clarity:

> The trend in modern times is to centralize more and more in London the intellectual, musical and artistic life of the nation. . . . There is now a very significant danger that the provinces will eventually be so heavily denuded of their talent, more particularly in music and drama, that they will become culturally barren and will not be able to supply the capital with the life-blood it needs. The BBC is rapidly becoming the most powerful and dominating organization in the cultural life of the country. It will soon be in a position to make or break provincial culture.[9]

The view from the provinces was that present BBC policy was tending to break, rather than make, provincial culture and the Regional Programme.

The regional production centres had been chosen not, in the first place, as the natural centres of some clearly bounded geo-graphical area with a particular identity of place and people, but as a rationalisation of already existing resources (the original 'main' stations) as the BBC moved to become a national service for the whole country. It had never been intended that the regions produce all or even most of their own material. By the mid-30s the amount each region produced varied from an upper limit of about 40 per cent from Midland, to a low of around 20 per cent, from Northern Ireland. This material was designed to fill the peak evening listening hours from 6.30 to 9.30. Daytime and late-night hours were largely filled by the overspill material transmitted on London Regional. There was a restricted system of networking whereby material from one region might be taken by others as part of their programme.

Material from the National Programme was also taken by the regions. A programme first broadcast by London might be repeated a few days later in the Regional Programme. This was known as 'diagonalisation'. London programmes were also, on occasion, transmitted simultaneously on the Regional Programme. There was a ratings system for these transmissions ranging from one to three stars. A three-star programme for simultaneous transmission meant it was of outstanding national importance and must be taken by the regions. A two-star programme was strongly recommended, and a one-star programme was recommended but not obligatory. Briggs gives a significant example of the conflicts which this ratings system could create. In 1934 a Sunday Symphony concert conducted by Casals was given a two-star rating. A. E. Harding, Director of Programmes in Manchester, had already planned to fill this slot in North Region's programme schedule with a concert by a group of unemployed musicians from Merseyside. A dialogue ensued, with London urging the cultural importance of Casals, and Harding urging the social significance of the Liverpool concert for his region. Harding stuck to his guns, and Manchester dropped the Casals concert.[10]

It took some years for a *modus vivendi* to be worked out between the two programmes. Crucially, it was not until the later 30s that it began to be appreciated in London that the Regional Programme might offer something different to the National Programme, and not merely the same only worse. The turning point was the *Report on Regions,* commissioned by the BBC in the aftermath of criticisms of its regional policy made to the Ullswater Committee (1936). The report, by Charles Siepmann (ex-Head of Talks, now Director of Regional Relations), declared that the policy of centralisation was short-sighted. The regions were the seedbed of talent and the ultimate source of supply of London's programmes. In particular Siepmann emphasised that the cultural standards which London took as the measure of the quality of its own works could not be applied to the regional service. The Regional Programme had a different rationale to that of the National Programme.

The report was read and accepted by senior management and the Board of Governors. The critique of centralisation was explicitly accepted and the Governors affirmed their support for the nurturing of local talent and the representation of local points of view. Local tastes in entertainment and culture (including music) should be met. All in all, the Governors believed that, in endorsing Siepmann's report, they were offering a Charter of Rights for the regional services. This marked a turning point in relations between the National and Regional Programmes and there was a remarkable growth of innovative and exciting programmes from the regions in the last few years before the outbreak of war.

National Regional and Local Broadcasting

It remains to consider the meaning of these arrangements and their definitions of the roles of national, regional and local broadcasting. Early BBC radio was genuinely local. The stations had a radius of twenty miles and largely drew upon local resources for their programmes. They were closely involved in their local community and had a relaxed, informal character very different from the tone of the system that replaced it. It was inevitable, however, that this system was not fully developed for both technical and economic reasons – although in saying this, it should be noted that it was inevitable *only* because of the BBC's monopoly and its emerging self-definition (and self-legitimation) as a national service.

It is as a national service first and foremost that the BBC has understood and defined its mission ever since 1927, and has been continuously reaffirmed in this self-definition by successive parliamentary reports, as well as White and Green Papers on broadcasting. The extent to which it has succeeded in this, the problems of expressing a national culture, the British way of life, raise major questions that go well beyond the scope of this short article. But one way of considering the problems involved in the manufacture of national cultural identity by broadcasting is to see how they were thrown into relief by regional broadcasting.

In the first place what was always presumed was the unity of the culture and identity of the United Kingdom, a presumption which glossed over its many disunities. There was the obvious problem of the two 'stateless nations' – Wales and Scotland – each being defined as mere regional adjuncts, not so much of England as of London. There was the particular problem of Northern Ireland – 'the most contrary region'[11] – whose implacable disunity fitted ill with the overall consensus sought by the BBC. Within England (an invisible term, actually, in the National/Regional scheme) the regional carve-up of the country (and why should not Wales or Scotland equally be subdivided?) can only be described as crudely oversimplified. There were in effect only three English regions:

North, Midland and West. There was a thing called London Regional, but it had no separate production centre or staff and transmitted 'overspill' material produced, in central London, by the staff of the National Programme.

Of the three English regional production centres the one with the clearest sense of a particular character rooted in place and people was North Region, based in Manchester.[12] West Region, based in Bristol (which has remained an important production centre for radio and television), was characterised by Siepmann as a quiet rural backwater and he considered recommending that it be closed down. Midland, based in Birmingham, was an important production centre with a higher output than any other region, but it was, as Siepmann noted, closer to London and London's outlook than anywhere else. As he remarked, the further away you got from London, the more independent or bloody-minded (depending on your point of view) the regions became.

It is difficult today to assess the effectiveness of the regional system, for although there have been studies of aspects of regional broadcasting in this period, there is not one that covers all regional production and output. But a contemporary assessment, at the end of the 30s, gives some indication of its emerging contribution to broadcasting. The author is Grace Wyndham Goldie, writing her last review as the *Listener's* often astringent radio critic:

> Let me before I die give one last shout about the importance of regional broadcasting. It is, I assure, worth shouting about. Its effect on English life is only just beginning to be felt and is already enormous. It is a side of broadcasting which I never see publicly discussed and the value of which I never see publicly recognized. . . . In London the search is for the best possible play, feature, actor, talk or entertainment and to provide it for listeners. But in the regions there is something else. For it is the business of regional broadcasting to be expressive of the region. It is its business to be a channel for regional talent. But there is more than that. For it is also the business of the regions to express the everyday life of the regions, its daily work, its past, its attitude of mind, and above all the quality of the people.[13]

Note that Goldie considers the impact of regional broadcasting on *English* life, a characteristic English habit of equating England with Britain. At the same time her response probably reflects the uneven impact of the different regions on national broadcasting as perceived from London. I think it fair to say that of all the pre-war regional centres it was Manchester that was most active and creative in programme-making in the late 30s. What was most clearly reflected in the differences between the output of Manchester and London were most generally those between North and South, a theme with a long history in English life and culture. Those differences were as much based on class as on differences of place. Manchester held together, not without difficulty, a sense of place and people in which perhaps working-class identity was the common factor among audiences drawn from many different localities (for example, the major towns and cities of Lancashire, Yorkshire and Tyneside), each with their own sense of local identity and pride. In the National Programme the ordinary life and experience of working people was marginal. It was central to North Region's programme service for its largely working-class audiences.

Goldie's last hurrah for regional broadcasting was more prescient than she realised. Six months later Britain was at war with Germany and the Regional Programme was closed down for security reasons. It was never revived. The National Programme continued as the Home Service (to distinguish it from the ever-increasing number of wartime Overseas Programmes) and was joined after a few months by the Forces Programme. This, at first an entertainment service for the British Expeditionary Force in France, became a more general entertainment programme for all British listeners after Dunkirk. The post-war radio service was a rationalisation of wartime broadcasting. Three national radio channels – the Light, Home and Third Programmes – reclassified the audience not in terms of differences of place and identity (local, regional, national) but in terms of broad differences of social and cultural tastes. The Light Programme (the new name for the wartime Forces Programme) was for lowbrows, and the wartime Home Service continued in peacetime as a programme for middlebrows. To these was added that 'uplift' service which BBC planners had occasionally yearned for since the mid-20s. The Third Programme was resolutely highbrow from its beginning in 1946.[14]

Within this scheme of things regional radio persisted in attenuated form through the 50s and most of the 60s as a networked sub-system of the Home Service. As television spread, it too set up studios and production facilities in the old regional centres. But television was developed from the start as a national service with the regional production centres and studios in the rest of the country producing material for national distribution or else making some local/regional input to news, current affairs, drama and documentaries. Today regionalism, in BBC parlance, refers to a substratum of national programme services. It no longer has, as it once enjoyed for a few years before the Second World War, an independent existence as a real alternative to national broadcasting.

* This chapter was first published in Sylvia Harvey and Kevin Robins (eds.), *The Regions, the Nations and the BBC* (London: BFI, 1993). My thanks to the BFI and to the author for permission to re-publish it in the present volume.

NOTES

1. BBC, *Extending Choice: The BBC's Role in the New Broadcasting Age* (London: BBC, 1992), p. 47.
2. A. Briggs, *The Birth of Broadcasting: The History of Broadcasting in the United Kingdom*, vol. 1 (Oxford: Oxford University Press, 1961), pp.216-19.
3. P. Eckersley, *The Power Behind the Microphone* (London: Jonathan Cape, 1941), pp. 69-70.
4. J. Reith, *Broadcast Over Britain* (London: Hodder & Stoughton, 1924), p.63.
5. P. Scannell and D. Cardiff, *A Social History of British Broadcasting. Vol. 1 'Serving the Nation, 1922-1939'* (Oxford: Basil Blackwell, 1991),pp.307-14.
6. A. Briggs, 'Local and regional in Northern sound broadcasting', *Northern History*, vol.10, 1975, p.173.
7. Eckersley, *The Power Behind the Microphone*, p.118.
8. BBC, *BBC Handbook* (London: BBC, 1929), p.57.
9. Scannell and Cardiff, *British Broadcasting*, p.336.
10. A. Briggs, *The Golden Age of Wireless: The History of Broadcasting in the United Kingdom*, vol. 2 (Oxford: Oxford University Press, 1965), p.328.
11. R. Cathcart, *The Most Contrary Region: The BBC in Northern Ireland, 1924-84* (Belfast: The Blackstaff Press, 1984).
12. Scannell and Cardiff, *British Broadcasting*, pp.333-55.
13. *Listener*, 6 March 1939.
14. K. Whitehead, *The Third Programme: A Literary History* (Oxford: Oxford University Press, 1989).

THE CONSTRUCTION OF A PARTITIONIST MENTALITY: EARLY BROADCASTING IN IRELAND

Martin McLoone

In his autobiography, León O Broin mentions an incident in August 1942 which illustrates very well the tensions that then existed between the two broadcasting organisations on the island – Radio Éireann in Dublin and the BBC in Belfast. One of Radio Éireann's most popular programmes was the quiz show, *Question Time,* hosted by Joe Linnane. As part of its policy to take the show 'on the road' outside of Dublin, Radio Éireann had requested and received permission from the BBC to do the show live from St. Mary's Hall in Belfast, using outside broadcast facilities. As O Broin tells it, a Belfast competitor was asked during the programme who was the best-known teller of fairy-tales, expecting the answer 'Hans Christian Andersen'. What he got, in fact, was 'Winston Churchill'.[1]

O'Broin had been a civil servant in Dublin throughout his career and spent twenty years in the Department of Posts and Telegraphs. In this capacity, he was very influential in the development of broadcasting in the South during the 1940's and 1950's and is therefore well placed to judge the importance of this incident on Dublin/Belfast relations. According to him, in Dublin the episode caused more amusement than embarrassment. In Belfast, however, according to Rex Cathcart, the reaction was very different.[2]

The Northern Ireland Director of the BBC at the time was George Marshall, a Scot who had forged a close relationship with the unionist establishment and whose broadcasting policy was designed around the principle of not giving offence to the unionist government and population. He had been forced by Head Office in London, against his own inclinations, to grant Radio Éireann permission to broadcast from Belfast for this edition of *Question Time.* Unionists were indignant about what had happened and the whole incident became an issue in the Belfast papers and was raised at Westminster. According to Cathcart, Marshall used the incident to insist that no further co-operation between Belfast and Dublin over outside broadcasts should take place for the duration of the war.[3]

The fact that these were the war years is significant for understanding the ferocity of unionist response to an incident which hardly raised an eye-brow in Dublin. The neutrality of the Free State was, for unionists, a clear example of the huge gap that now existed between the two states and it reinforced their view that Dublin was untrustworthy, cowardly and anti-British in the most treacherous manner. Whatever London might think (and the BBC was responding to British government pressure to keep relationships between the two broadcasting organisations cordial and supportive) there was an unbridgeable difference in priorities which, for unionists and therefore for Marshall, made co-operation dangerous and potentially treacherous. To some extent, of course, this difference in priorities was true.

In the early 1940's, for example, there were constant complaints in the Dáil about the fact the main news bulletins on Radio Éireann led with the war news and the Irish items were fitted in afterwards. As one Dáil Deputy (Brendan Corish, Labour) argued in 1941:

I think it was a week last Monday that Cardinal MacRory made a statement about his pastoral being held up and that was almost the last item in the news. All the English war news was given before it. Surely the Minister does not suggest that for Irish listeners the war news was more important than Cardinal MacRory's statement?[4]

By this time, what is effectively 'a partitionist mentality' had been well sedimented on both sides of the border and the differing priorities during the war were a manifestation of this, rather than the cause. Two famous judgements of broadcasting on both sides of the border at this time confirm the extent of cultural polarisation. Writing of Radio Éireann in the decades following its establishment in 1926, Maurice Gorham observed:

It was expected not merely to reflect every aspect of national activity, but to create activities which did not exist. It was

expected to revive the speaking of Irish; to foster a taste for classical music; to revive Irish traditional music; to keep people on
the farms; to sell goods and services of all kinds from sausages
to sweep tickets; to provide a living and a career for writers and
musicians; to reunite the Irish people at home with those overseas; to end partition.[5]

During the 1930's and early 1940's, the political and cultural
expression of Irish nationalism on radio took on a particularly de
Valera-ian hue and de Valera himself consciously used radio as a
means of promoting his own political and ideological agenda,
much to the chagrin of the opposition in the Dáil.[6] Thus the development of broadcasting in the south was hitched, perhaps not surprisingly, to a cultural agenda defined by Fianna Fáil.

In 1936, the BBC's Director of Regional Relations, Charles
Siepmann, visited Belfast as part of a fact-finding tour of all the
BBC regions. His report on Northern Ireland, contained in a
lengthy appendix to his main report, is particularly scathing of the
BBC's Belfast operation. Noting the political context in which the
BBC operated, he described it as nothing less 'than a loyalist dictatorship'. He drew a parallel between the grandiose pretensions
of government in Northern Ireland and its rather favoured broadcasting provision.

A system of government developed by and for a great nation has
been imposed on a province the size of Yorkshire and a population a little larger than that of Glasgow. . . . Broadcasting in
Northern Ireland is necessitated by political considerations. It is
not justified by any extent of indigenous programme resources.[7]

Siepmann went on to excoriate the quality of locally-produced
programmes and to lament the poverty of the talent and creativity
which the BBC had to draw on. What he did not comment on was
that, in its Director, George Marshall, it had a man unwilling to
antagonise the unionist establishment, thus effectively recruiting
the BBC on behalf of Siepmann's 'loyalist dictatorship'. Indeed,
Cathcart even suggests that Marshall kept in close contact with the
Northern Ireland Prime Minister over broadcasting matters, a situation made possible by his membership of the Ulster Club. By
the beginning of the war, he had established his right of veto over
the whole of the BBC network in regard to programming about

the whole of Ireland, and not just about or within his Northern Ireland region. And though, on occasion, he could resist unionist or Protestant pressure on some issues (for example, over coverage of the Twelfth of July processions and speeches), nonetheless, Cathcart's judgement is that 'what increasingly manifests itself is his inclination to line up with the unionist position vis-à-vis the Irish Free State/Éire'[8]

The broadcasting systems in the north and the south had, by this time, settled into a partitionist pattern, the one depending on, and reacting to the other. It is tempting, indeed, to see this relationship as symbiotic and there is certainly an argument to be made that in terms of the development of broadcasting in the south, there has always been a close correlation with, and a reaction to, developments in the north. There can be no doubt that the opening of the BBC's Belfast station (2BE) in September 1924 gave a sense of urgency to the debates in the south regarding a station for the Free State. This was a pattern followed in the 1950s in regard to the establishing of an Irish television service. By this time, over thirty per cent of the population in the south could receive pictures from BBC NI and UTV and this provided an added incentive to get a local Irish station started. Even as late as the 1970s, the proposal of the Minister, Conor Cruise O' Brien, to relay BBC1 as a second channel on RTE stimulated a heated debate about the need for a second Irish channel, eventually leading to the setting up of RTE 2 (now called Network 2).

To understand the relationship between the BBC in Belfast and Radio Éireann (originally 2RN) in Dublin, it is important to look at the early years of broadcasting developments. For, as Rex Cathcart points out, it took time for the social, economic and cultural implications of partition to impinge on people [9] and reading the historical documents and newspapers of the 1920s and early 1930s confirms this. In the cultural arena, the debates about broadcasting, north and south, give an insight into the way in which the partitionist mentality evolves. The polarisation evident by the 1940s was not anticipated in the earliest years of broadcasting. Indeed, some of the early omens seemed to bode well.

In October 1925, a Civil Service Commission selection board was held in Dublin to appoint a director for the new Free State station and John Reith himself sat on this as an advisor. Having failed to appoint at this time, the board met again the following month and Reith sent over a senior BBC figure, Roger Eckersley, to represent him. In these early years there is little doubt that the BBC in general helped the new Dublin operation in many practical and technical matters and by October 1927, Reith could opine, in a letter of congratulations to the Dublin-based *Irish Radio Review:*

> On the occasion of your second birthday, I would like to wish continued success and prosperity to broadcasting in the Free State. While the primary mission of broadcasting is to serve the people, it has also – and perhaps in no less a degree – to serve the peoples, and the programme arrangements now in force between the Irish organisation and our own are not only an index of our happy relations, but a beginning of the still wider interchange which is foreshadowed in the BBC motto: 'Nation shall speak peace unto Nation'.[10]

In fact, the *Irish Radio Journal,* the *Review's* competitor, had itself editorialised these sentiments on a number of occasions during the two years before Reith's letter was published. In its New Year message of January 1927, the editorial declared sonorously:

> Above all do we hold that radio and wireless broadcasting will help to bring the nations closer and closer together, and thus make for that material respect and sympathy, that understanding and appreciation, which will herald that age of Peace for which the world has sighed so often and hitherto sighed in vain.[11]

Even earlier, in April 1926, it addressed the Belfast/Dublin relationship specifically:

> We have had our initial relay from the Northern Ireland Athens, and Belfast is to have one from us. This is good. All the intercourse that can be established between the two cities must be welcome. We want no barriers and broadcasting may be a potent influence in bringing the two great civic communities closer and closer together.[12]

As it turned out, this was all wishful thinking. Perhaps the experience at the Ulster Hall in Belfast on the night of the BBC's formal opening on 24 October 1924 was a more reliable indication of the cultural polarisation which was to follow. As Cathcart describes it: 'A range of dignitaries from the new establishment attended and revealed their political disposition by breaking into loud cheers and laughter when the London news bulletin, which was relayed into the Hall, announced the arrest of Eamonn de Valera by the RUC in Newry.'[13]

Over the next few years, debates about the cultural role and likely impact of broadcasting revolved around three areas. First, there was a constant debate over the amount of dance music (often referred to, pejoratively, as 'jazz') on the wireless and this quickly became a discussion about 'highbrow' and 'lowbrow' tastes in general. To be fair, this was part of a much wider debate, throughout the UK and in the Free State,[14] but it developed a particular resonance in Northern Ireland when linked to two other sources of controversy, the definition of 'Irishness' which was seen to predominate on the BBC in general, and in Belfast in particular, and a contrasting definition of 'Ulster' identity which came to dominate general unionist thinking as the implications of partition began to sink in.

These three controversies hinged on the relationship between the BBC in Belfast and Headquarters in London and on the question of local autonomy. This was a sore point with many people right from the beginning, given that the Belfast station was originally managed and run by non-Northern Irish personnel. The question of local input and the advantages of local knowledge had become an issue even before the BBC opened in Belfast. Six months before the opening, the Northern correspondent of the *Irish Radio Journal* noted acerbically:

The announcer at the London station caused great amusement to Northern listeners recently by the attempts which he made to pronounce Fermanagh. Lectures from Irish stations on the orthoëpy of Irish names should be given for the benefit of officials of English stations. It is hoped that these lectures will be given before Doagh qualifies for a place in the news bulletins.[15]

However, the matter of orthoëpy was the least of unionist concerns, as the BBC operation got under way. Over the next few years, the nature of the St. Patrick Day broadcasts, both locally and on the network, became the focus of intense debate. The problem was the definition of 'Irishness' which the broadcasts assumed, and the increasing polarisation of unionist opinion on the matter can be mapped out by the reaction to each year's celebratory programmes. Rex Cathcart points out that after the first year of the BBC's Belfast programming, in 1925, there was no reaction but from 1926 onwards, the nature of these special programmes gave rise to an increasingly acrimonious debate. When the listings from the Belfast station for that year's St. Patrick's Day broadcast first appeared, they were criticised by the nationalist press, which noted that other regions of the BBC were marking the day with a greater Irish content than Belfast. The programme was hurriedly changed to include more Irish items but then, at the last moment, a proposed relay from Dublin was cancelled without explanation. Cathcart surmises that someone in (political?) authority in Belfast put pressure on London to have the Dublin items cut above the heads of the Belfast staff. 'The events of St. Patrick's Day 1926 provide a paradigm of the future', he concludes.[16]

The central issue in these controversies is the very reason for having the special programmes in the first place. As Scannell and Cardiff argue, the St. Patrick's Day programmes were part of a continuing process of marking out and celebrating the different constituents of a national culture, making, to use Reith's own phrase, 'the nation as one man'.

> Nothing so well illustrates the noiseless manner in which the BBC becomes the central agent of national culture as its calendrical role; the cyclical reproduction, year in year out, of an orderly and regular progression of festivities, rituals and celebrations – major and minor, civil and sacred – that marked the unfolding of the broadcast year.[17]

St. Patrick's Day was to be an important element in this annual cycle. In Northern Ireland, it was to be anything but 'noiseless'. My own feeling about the lack of controversy in the first year, 1925, is that there were two factors at play. First, at this early stage, there was still a lack of perspective on partition; still a tendency not to see the border or to fully grasp the implications of its existence. Reading contemporary documents it is obvious that after one hundred years of co-habitation, the practical and cultural implications of the divorce of Belfast from Dublin (or Dublin from London) were slow to impinge. This was as true in Ireland, north and south, as it was in Britain itself but once broadcasting became more involved in constructing a 'national' culture, the symbolic representations of nationality were bound to become more controversial. Second, of course, is the fact that by 1926, the Free State service was up and running and its commitment to a specific sense of Irish national culture was to provide a focus for debates in the north. As Cathcart has shown, during the 1930s, many of the unifying 'national' events, including the regional messages of goodwill before the King's Christmas address, became increasingly more acrimonious as a result.[18]

The unionist argument was that the lack of Ulster expertise in the BBC in Belfast and a general inclination of London to view 'Irishness' within a broadly 'nationalist' cultural agenda constantly misrepresented unionist, Protestant identity. Cathcart quotes, among many outraged unionist listeners over these years, a letter to the *Belfast News Letter* of 30 December 1933, on the subject of the recent Christmas day broadcast:

> We are cut off from the rest of Ireland by the border. We have not anything to do with it and we never will have. Erin is Ireland. Ireland is on the other side of the border: yet we hear the voice of Ulster proclaiming in song, 'Come back to Erin'. Ye Gods! Think of it. . . . Many people have thought for a long time that there is too much of the Irish pipe, the Irish jig and the Irish atmosphere in the BBC programmes from Belfast.[19]

What affronted another letter-writer on the same topic was the thought that the King himself had to listen to this version of Irishness!

It has to be said though that there was a degree of confusion over exactly what it was the unionists were objecting to and what it was they wanted in terms of more acceptable representations of their Ulster identity. On one hand there is a clear rejection of the Irishness represented by what they saw as primarily nationalist culture, the implication being that Ulster identity formed an alternative version of 'Irishness'. On the other hand, there was also a desire for the Britishness of Ulster to be recognised as no different to the Britishness of London and in many regards, this expression of 'Malone Road' Britishness was apt to reject the culture and accents of the working-class Protestant and the rural Ulsterman as easily as it did the southerner. At this point the issue of class, which lay behind the debates over classical music and jazz, enters the debate over cultural identity. What unites these divergent, even contradictory, inclinations is the desire to see more local input into the running of the operation – a call for more local autonomy from the centre. There is, then, an irony in the fact that the loyal unionist sought to break free from the centralised control of the Imperial centre, which could not be trusted to guarantee proper representation for its loyal subjects. On the other hand, the expression of Catholic, Irish cultural identity was more likely in a BBC under the firm control of London, with its more liberal political and cultural ethos and, it has to be admitted, its insensitivity to the unionist dilemma.[20] In the figure of George Marshall, the unionists at least got an outsider who worked assiduously to protect their interests from the insensitive centre and the hostile forces across the border.

The other side of the coin to all this was, of course, the direction in which broadcasting south of the border was developing and like the situation with the BBC in Belfast, perhaps the early signs of openness and accommodation were deceptive. From the earliest debates about broadcasting in the south, it is obvious that its cultural role in nation-building was to take precedence over its potential for international co-operation. In May 1925, after nearly two years of debate in the south about the proposed broadcasting station, the *Irish Radio Journal* could quote Disraeli approvingly: 'Individuals may form communities, but it is institutions alone that can create a nation'.[21]

In reference to this period, the playwright Lennox Robinson wrote that for the future historian, three official government reports of the time would prove invaluable – the Accounts Committee Report, the Report of the Army Inquiry and the Wireless Broadcasting Report. 'These three Reports furnish the secret history of Ireland from 1921 to 1926', he asserted. He was writing about his recently-deceased friend, Major Bryan Cooper, who sat as an independent in the first Free State Dáil and who played a significant part in the Dáil debates about these Reports.[22] In fact Robinson is certainly correct about the wireless debate and it is obvious from the records that broadcasting came to be recognised as one of the more important institutions for nation-building. The debate was not really over this fact, but over the nature of the nation which it was to assist in building. If the evolution of a partitionist mentality in the north can be mapped out in Belfast through the debates about the BBC's calendrical marking of a

national culture, the same can be done for the annual debate in
the Dáil over the broadcasting estimates. The key early debates
took place in February 1924, when the Special Committee, set up
by the Dáil to investigate and recommend the best mechanism for
establishing and managing a broadcasting station, reported its
findings.

At this time, the Dáil had still not legalised wireless ownership
but thousands of Irish people owned receivers illegally and were
already tuning into the BBC and other services. The Irish
Postmaster General, J. J. Walsh, had already published a White
Paper proposing that the station be run as a private concession
under the control of Irish companies (following the model of the
BBC at that time, an Irish Broadcasting Company) but the Special
Committee recommended that the state should own and manage
the station in the national interest and that in the interim, while
the new service was being established, licences be issued immediately to allow for the legal ownership of wireless receivers. In dis-
cussing the Committee's recommendations, Walsh asked the Dáil
to reconsider both of these proposals. 'We have legalised law
breakers. We have deprived this country of a broadcasting station;
we have turned it over to British music hall dope and British propaganda . . . ', he asserted, so setting the tone and character of the
debate which was to follow.[23]

What is interesting in Walsh's response is that the rather technical matter of how the station should be set up and managed is
conflated with the role that broadcasting is to play in the national
interest and again, how the cultural aspect of this national interest
must clearly distinguish itself from the wireless culture of Britain.
As in the debates in Belfast, there is, implicit in Walsh's statement,
a fear of popular forms of culture ('music hall dope') and a recognition of the ideological power of the new medium ('propaganda'), both of which, because of the already looming presence
of the BBC, he then identifies as British. It is these aspects which
are picked up in the ensuing debate in the Dáil and which begin
to dominate general press coverage of the issue.

The Deputy for Carlow/Kilkenny, D. J. Gorey, for example,
opines that broadcasting 'in the future may develop into one of
the greatest elements of our national life . . . almost as important
in a national and moral sense as our schools.' This further
conflates the national with the religious and the cultural parameters of the national culture which broadcasting is to support are

further defined when he references recent debates in the Dáil about the dangers of film. 'We do not want the minds of our youths contaminated with some of the stuff that the youths of other countries have been imbibing. . . . I quite agree with the Postmaster-General's statement . . . that we ought to be careful not to make this country an English shire.' While a conflation of American film and 'jazz' with all that an 'English shire' might connote beggars belief today, it is important to realise that the opinions of Walsh and Gorey are in no way at the extreme of contemporary opinion in Ireland at this time. This is why Lennox Robinson's assertion that this debate gives an insight into the mood of the times is correct. In this debate, as in many others about broadcasting over the next quarter century, these attitudes are the accepted ideological norm. Disagreement here is about how best the ideals are to be met in regard to broadcasting (state control or Irish private enterprise) and difference of opinion later is in relation to how well 2RN or Radio Éireann performs its national role. That role and the ideological character of the task is rarely in dispute.

The exception in the debate of 1924 was Bryan Cooper, the subject of Robinson's biography. His intervention on 15 February is particularly telling. His was a witty and entertaining speech, but also deeply significant and prescient. Cooper, of course, was an Anglo-Irish Protestant with an estate in Sligo and before the war, he had represented South Dublin in Westminster as a Unionist MP. Robinson praises his liberal and open attitude to independence and particularly congratulates him on his contribution to the early operations of the Free State Dáil. In retrospect, though, his voice was that of a declining political force and his liberal accommodation with the running tide of nationalism was echoed in few other places. But his arguments do have a strangely contemporary air and provide a telling contrast to the hardening partitionist mentality evident in the broadcasting debate in both the north and the south.

Picking up on Walsh's phrase 'British music hall dope and British propaganda', he offers a more high-cultural definition of what the BBC offered (*Hamlet*, *Parsifal* and the music of Glazounov were to be broadcast that evening, he noted). He worried about the nature of 'Irishness' which Walsh seemed to want. 'I am afraid that if we are to have wireless established on a exclusively Irish-Ireland basis, the result will be "Danny Boy" four times a week, with varia-

tions by way of camouflage.' He finished his contribution with a
plea that is uncannily prescient of similar debates in the 1990s:

> It is my very deep and profound conviction . . . that we cannot
> set up a Chinese wall around the country, or establish an exclu-
> sive civilisation. If we wish to do that, let there be no wireless
> broadcasting, let there be no telegraphic cables, no foreign
> postal service. If we are to pursue that policy, let us pursue it to
> its logical conclusion. We are not a little island in the middle of
> the Atlantic between America and Europe. For good or evil, we
> are a part of Europe. In the past – the distant past – we
> influenced Europe profoundly and I hope it will be our lot to do
> so again. We shall not do it by pursuing a policy of isolation and
> by shutting out the education that comes from European civili-
> sation.[25]

In a later debate in the Dáil, on 3 April, Cooper launched an
attack on the narrow moralism and self-denying asceticism surrounding the whole question. 'The Postmaster-General is a little
too virtuous for the ordinary man. He thinks, because he is virtuous, we should take no more cakes and ale.'[26](Walsh was opposed
to the broadcasting of racing results and eighteen months later, in
speaking to the first estimates following the setting up of 2RN, he
declared his intention of shutting down the station at 10.30 each
evening; 'I consider that it is a bad practice to take people off the
normal track of living; to keep them up late at night and to disturb
the usual routine of life unduly.')[27] Cooper's vision of a cultural
'Chinese wall' is exactly what the Dáil was constructing through
the legislation on the censorship of films and literature and
through its definition of 'Irishness', evident in the broadcasting
debate. Cooper died in 1930 and so was not to witness the new
momentum given to this policy of cultural isolation under the de
Valera governments from 1932 on. But in truth, his liberal sentiments and his promotion of a European sense of identity had few
supporters, either north or south of the border, and had to wait
many generations before it would find a place on the cultural
agenda. Rather, the general tenor of the debate confirms that
there was a surprising unanimity on all political sides on the sense
of Irishness which broadcasting was to support and its insular and
at times xenophobic nature was clearly articulated even at this
early stage.

By way of summary, I want to return to the debate in Belfast. It is obvious that the national role being designed and constructed in the south had an impact on the north and the experience of the BBC in Belfast in turn gave the debate in the south an added charge. In this way, broadcasting was used to copper-fasten the partitionist mentality and though it is to overstate the case to single out broadcasting as the decisive factor in this process, nonetheless, its role was extremely significant. It is interesting, though, to note some of the ironies and contradictions in the position which broadcasting found itself on both sides of the border. In their attacks on the BBC in Belfast, unionists called for a contradictory policy. Middle-class unionist opinion was quite happy to see Northern Ireland represented as 'an English shire' and was as unhappy with the northern vernacular as it was with southern accents. There was, however, an equally impassioned plea for a more vernacular version of Ulster, one that reflected the Protestant culture which distinguished Northern Ireland from both the Free State and the rest of the UK. This opinion, in effect, looked for the BBC to construct a cultural 'Chinese wall' around the border to keep out the 'foreign' culture that lay to the south. Equally, 'foreign' culture in the south was sometimes synonymous with 'British' and this gave rise to a culture of sullen and antagonistic suspicion, especially where more popular forms of culture were concerned.

Yet, centrally, the BBC tended to regard the BBC in Belfast as the BBC in Ireland and its version of 'Irishness' was closely aligned to what would have been commonly regarded as 'nationalist'. The unionist call for more local voices and greater local control was really a reflection of the mistrust felt about the BBC and its seeming inability to deliver a unionist sense of 'Irishness' or 'Britishness'. Nationalist opinion, on the other hand, tended to demand a greater involvement by London in the affairs of the BBC in Belfast, sensing, quite rightly, that this was the only way to guarantee a fair reflection of Irish identity. Indeed, over the years, the Irishness of the BBC's programmes was often cited in the south in criticism of the performance of 2RN/Radio Éireann. There can be no doubt that where it was appropriate, either for the network or BBC NI, there was a fair representation of general 'Irishness' on the BBC and this continued to be a bone of contention for unionists. However, as Marshall established his powers of veto over the whole of the BBC in relation to Ireland, this sense of 'Irishness' was considerably circumscribed to avoid offending unionists as much as possible and every attempt was made to ensure that this sense of identity was located south of the border. Nationalist culture in Northern Ireland was an altogether different matter, and the banning of GAA results from being broadcast on Sundays and the lack of any Irish language programmes at all, is indicative of the prevailing attitude that, no matter about the culture south of the border, it had little relevance to the north. Above all, for Marshall, there should be no expression of political opposition to the Northern Ireland state itself.

The final irony, of course, is that despite the concerted efforts made in both states, broadcasting could not be contained within one state or the other, and could never successfully be constrained within an exclusive and narrow identity. American dance music and popular culture of all kinds continued to be the mainstay of general programming and if the market research of those companies which sponsored programmes on 2RN is to be believed, then the popular audience preferred the less lofty and less idealistic programming anyway. While the attempt to control radio for an essentially conservative cultural policy was no doubt successful in both states for a time, nonetheless, radio was also a mechanism for modernisation and for slowly opening up the narrowness of the cultural agenda which was being set. Broadcasting may have helped to forge a partitionist mentality in the first place but it was also slowly undermining the cultural assumptions which underpinned it. This was to reach its culmination by the late 1960s in the hugely influential role played by television in undermining the unionist state and in throwing the complacent certainties of southern Irish nationalism into considerable disarray.

NOTES
1. León O Broin, *Just like Yesterday* (Dublin: Gill and Macmillan, 1985), p.190.
2. Rex Cathcart, *The Most Contrary Region: The BBC in Northern Ireland 1924-1984* (Belfast: Blackstaff Press, 1984), p.124.
3. ibid., p.125.
4. *Dáil Debates*, 4 June 1941, vol.83, col.1531.
5. Maurice Gorham, *Forty Years of Irish Broadcasting* (Dublin: Talbot Press, 1967).
6. Martin McLoone, 'Inventions and Re-imaginings: Some thoughts on Identity and Broadcasting in Ireland' in Martin McLoone (ed.), *Culture, Identity and Broadcasting in Ireland* (Belfast: Inst. of Irish Studies, 1991). p.13.
7. Rex Cathcart, *The Most Contrary Region*, pp.2-5 and 78-82.
8. ibid., p.91.

9. ibid., p.60.
10. *Irish Radio Review,* vol.3, no.1, October 1927, p.1.
11. *Irish Radio Journal,* 1 January 1927, p.2207.
12. ibid., 7 April 1926.
13. Rex Cathcart, *The Most Contrary Region,* p.25.
14. Paddy Scannell and David Cardiff, *A Social History of British Broadcasting, Volume 1 1922-39* (Oxford: Blackwell, 1991), pp.205-223.
15. 'Northern Notes', *Irish Radio Journal,* March 1924.
16. Rex Cathcart, *The Most Contrary Region,* p.34.
17. Paddy Scannell and David Cardiff, *A Social History of British Broadcasting,* p.278.
18. Rex Cathcart, *The Most Contrary Region,* pp.60-106.
19. ibid., p.66.
20. For a fuller discussion of this see, Martin McLoone, 'A Little Local Difficulty? Public Service Broadcasting, Regional Identity and Northern Ireland' in Sylvia Harvey and Kevin Robins (eds.) *The Regions, the Nations and the BBC* (London: BFI, 1993), pp.38-48.
21. *Irish Radio Journal,* 1 May 1925.
22. Lennox Robinson, *Bryan Cooper* (London: Constable, 1931), p.163.
23. *Dáil Debates,* 14 February 1924, vol.6, col.1085.
24. ibid., 15 February 1924, cols.1112-13.
25. ibid., cols.1116-20. For another discussion of this see, Martin McLoone, 'Inventions and Re-imaginings' pp.2-30.
26. ibid., 3 April 1924, col.2883.
27. ibid., 28 January 1926, vol.14, cols.267-79.

FROM PORTLAND STONE TO THE RIVER FOYLE: THE DECENTRALISING AND DEMOCRATISING OF BBC RADIO

Des Cranston

Let there be no ambiguity: it is wireless broadcasting that provides the continuity for the seventy years of the BBC in Northern Ireland. I should like, therefore, to concentrate on what I would argue to have been the gradual decentralisation and democratisation of radio broadcasting during those seventy years. I propose to discuss some of the influences on the BBC in NI with reference to the output of the past. I should also like to examine the introduction and development of regional and local radio with reference to some recently released archive material.

Much time and energy has been, and continues to be, devoted to analysing news and current affairs, especially that of the past twenty-five years. Tensions that traditionally had been shared privately among broadcasters are now, quite properly, matters of public debate. The 'bias and rudeness' of radio interviewers are today of sufficient concern to be discussed in the press. A survey of listeners to the *Today* programme, for example, led recently to the headline 'Listeners support Humphrys' and a full profile of John Humphry's style and approach appeared in the same issue of *The Observer* under the heading 'A terrier who bites his way through Waffle'.[1]

The cessation of twenty-five years of armed violence has produced an anticipated outcome; uncertainty. This is a challenge that radio had to come to terms with once before, in the huge and sudden shifts in societal norms after the end of the Second World War. As the BBC Yearbook noted at the time, 'War reporting had one thing about it that spelt simplicity. There was seldom much difference of opinion on any given week, as to what was the right lead for the news.'[2] There is, of course, an uncontested assumption implicit in this statement about the fixed nature of the criteria setting the dominant news agenda. As television transmission had been suspended during the Second World War, radio had established its special position between 1939-45 and made itself as an indispensable part of the social fabric. Throughout the whole of Europe, the BBC had become a source of information that was trusted. Of course, the recent experience of Northern Ireland is on a much smaller scale and differs in some other fundamental ways – not only in the number of radio sources available and the added visual input of television, but also because analysis and interpretation now constitutes the majority of the running time of news programmes and there is little evidence of there being much uncontested ground there.

Nonetheless, many of the current debates within and about broadcasting in general, and about television in particular, have been rehearsed about radio in the past. The tensions between 'The Administration' (retitled 'Management') and programme-makers and their staff, did not surface, suddenly, with the arrival of Hussey or Birt. For example, the late RD Smith, formerly a producer with BBC Drama and Features and Professor of Liberal and Contemporary Studies at Magee College, once remarked in an interview about Radio Features, 'For a short time administrators had to support creative writers.'[3] Occasionally differences of emphasis or interpretation would cause programmes to be banned. Fifty years before *At the Edge of the Union* (1985) D.G. Bridson's *Prometheus*, produced in Manchester, was banned by London as its content was thought to be subversive. As Bridson said later in an interview, 'The idea that workers could become militant if things were sufficiently bad for them was regarded to be highly suspect'.[4] In 1961, long before the debates about *The Monocled Mutineer* and *Tumbledown*, Louis MacNeice's political radio play about South Africa, *The Pin is Out* had been banned. It has been described as 'a satire against racist Fascism as bitter as Orwell's against Communism'.[5] It was rejected by the Director of Sound Broadcasting because, 'its effect must be to attack a Commonwealth Government at a particularly difficult moment in Commonwealth relations'.[6] As Philip Donovan observed, 'The BBC believed that audiences should be soothed, not excited.'[7].

For 50 years, local output in Northern Ireland was dominated by the national, metropolitan-centred Britishness of the BBC. The UK was not unique in this centralised focus of broadcasting. Even a cursory review of the relationship between notions of national identity and broadcasting (India, China, the African states after independence) will provide dozens of examples. In Europe, Hitler had harnessed the media to promote National Socialism. In the USA, despite a fragmented, local and commercialised system, the New Deal was presented through a series of radio-broadcast 'fireside chats'. And in Britain at the same time, Chamberlain was aware that through the mass media, an image could be constructed. As Ken Ward notes, 'By 1938 Chamberlain had constructed an image of an international statesman, by the use of newsreels, the press and broadcasting.'[8] It is important to remember that such broadcasts were received nationally – there was no 'opting-out' available to the regions. Constitutionally, in 1931 the Empire had become The Commonwealth but by 1939 it was evident that the spirit of the Empire was striking back, if indeed, it had ever gone away. The nation was being united: centralism, not regionalism, was the order of the day. The style of the time is encapsulated in Anthony Eden's response to there having been a Nazi salute given at a meeting of the League of Nations in Geneva, 1936 (reported on *Radio Gazette*), 'We did not see any incident and if there was one, it would be more in keeping with our dignity if we did not notice it.'[9]

That sense of distance from reality was reinforced by the remoteness of the BBC. An appropriate illustration of this can be heard in the total lack of drama, indeed of interest, in the live commentary from the west terrace of the Crystal Palace during the fire. A bored voice hoped, 'For an expert. . . Ah, here is an expert', who then described, above the noise, the scene of the fire moving at 5 yards a second, the crashing glass. The reporter broke in with, 'We can't keep you here all night,' clearly his time and ours was being wasted. Later that evening the sports news reported that, 'The match between Clapton Orient and Crystal Palace was postponed because of fog.' (sic).[10] The Reithian trinity of informing, educating and entertaining was secure in the arts – the Best Play of the Year (1936) was Professor Gilbert Murray's translation of the Hippolytus of Euripides.

It was into this BBC of evening dress and the London smart scene, epitomised by the music and style of *Henry Hall's Guest Night,* that the BBC Features Department (Northern Region) in Manchester erupted. It gave access to the voices of ordinary people of the north of England. Poetry and journalism; dramatic form and documentary style were synthesised; the Feature programme emerged.

1936 was significant for the Northern Ireland Region. The commissioning of the Lisnagarvey transmitter in March, meant that programmes could be received outside the immediate Belfast area. The result was that the majority of the Northern Ireland audience could receive clearly the whole BBC programme rather than the poor quality long wave reception of national programmes. But the problems of reception and wavelengths had not been satisfactorily resolved; this issue that would appear again. In the same year the BBC commissioned Charles Siepmann to undertake an investigation into the regions of the Corporation. His Report on the Regions carried a supplement on Northern Ireland. While he encouraged the Features output, he excoriated the drama output, especially the kitchen comedy. (How would he have reacted to *The McCooeys* huge success 20 years later?)

One debate crossed the Irish Sea and found resonance in Northern Ireland. Class distinction was manifested in the acceptable speech style of a Received Pronunciation (R.P.) accent. R.P., the educated Oxford vowel sounds, pronunciation and modulated intonation which characterised upper-class delivery, provided the expected norm for broadcasters. Manchester's output had challenged that expectation. (Like several areas of debate about broadcasting, accent and style continue to be hotly contested areas even today. Radio 4's popular *Feedback* programme of 24 March 1995 was devoted entirely to listeners' and broadcasters' views on regional accents on national programmes.) Siepmann's recommendation to encourage local talent seemed to support local accents, and with them, the use of dialect speech. But the controlled production methods of the time clearly were at odds with that objective. Even Joan Littlewood, who was to give such vitality to the theatre in Stratford East, had, to the Northern Ireland ear, a very upper-class accent and style when interviewing. While her interviewees were recorded in the factory, the recordings had to be written down and then read by the worker, often in the alien world of the studio. It was significant that these experiments were happening in the regions. DG. Bridson had no doubts why: 'Because the regions were comparatively free from administrative interference.'[11]

Children's Hour had a local input, including the popular 'I want to be an actor' spot, but the voices that dominated many childhoods were those of its presenter, Uncle Mac and the upper-class delivery of Larry the Lamb in the long-running *Toytown* series. The juxtaposition of the speech of actors in Northern Ireland plays and the R.P. announcers at BBC headquarters in Ormeau Avenue sat together uneasily. Not until the arrival of the independent commercial station Downtown Radio (16 March, 1976) were radio contributors and station announcers clearly from the same region.

The BBC Northern Ireland Region was, therefore, up until the Second World War, an integral part of the dominant political, class, and business structure. There is nothing remarkable about that. 'We assumed that a close relationship existed among Musgrave Street, Glengall Street, Stormont, and a clutch of big business families, after all, it was only common sense to secure the state.'[12]. As there were few locally produced programmes, during the War there was no regional development, except for the engineers at the Lisnagarvey transmitter which became a key link in the international shortwave network.[13]. In 1940 the Controller (Programmes) sent a memo to all regions requiring that the Northern Ireland Director should be consulted about programmes that discussed either Northern Ireland or Eire.[14] In effect, the Northern Ireland region had established a unique role within the BBC, a role that it was to reassert thirty years later when the Troubles began again.

The Northern Ireland listener, in common with the rest of the U.K., continued to hear an output dominated by London. While programmes were predominately studio-based, (R.P. accents communicating the staggering events of the time) the influence and success of the work of North Region had radically influenced broadcasting. The actuality recordings of the Features Department had come a long way from the woeful account of the Crystal Palace fire. Listening now, to recordings made in bombers as they flew through flak; or to *Worker's Playtime*, which began in 1941; or to the down-to-earth concerns of women in the duologues of two characters, Gert and Daisy and to the confidential tones of the Radio Doctor, ('How's the tongue today? Are you ignoring the whispering message of the lower bowel?') argues strongly that those who were actively involved were at least as interesting as the professional broadcasters. But class divisions were never far away, *The Brains Trust* was asked 'What is meant by national culture?' and could answer confidently, 'Personality. The Greeks didn't have it'. Churchill looked forward to post-war

Britain, 'To a Britain that will need to draw her leaders from every type of school and wearing every kind of tie'.[15]

When the regions were re-established after the war, one of Siepmann's recommendations was acted upon and the Features Department was reopened. Sam Hanna Bell recalls Louis MacNeice's visits to Ormeau Avenue in 1945, the first to supervise the setting up of the Department and then to produce W.R. Rogers' *City Set on a Hill* in November 1945. Looking back, little change to the local output is apparent. The regional pattern was being set for the next 30 years. However, the BBC's status had been enhanced during the War, and there was a natural transfer of that to the Region. Upper class accents sustained the pre-war style; Ormeau Avenue was a very prestigious place to work. The secretaries, like those we hear in excerpts of pre-war reminiscence, were 'ladies'. At the BBC silver Jubilee celebrations at Hillsborough in 1949, they were told to wear hats and gloves and to dress conservatively 'and not to outshine the guests'.[16] But reading the content of the radio programme is a rather dispiriting exercise today.

The new era was heralded by a schedule packed with nostalgia for a pre-war lyricism; for an imagined Northern Ireland not for the real one. W.R. Rogers *The Return Room*, read by Denys Hawthorne, was a romantic recall of the 1930's : 'Spring. The one time in the year when the stranger was welcome within our gates.' There are lines that predate Dylan Thomas, 'We ran weightless through the barelegged streets.'[17]. Nellie Wheeler remembered acting with the Ulster Literary theatre in the '20s; Lynn Doyle philosophised from Devon; and, what continues to be a contemporary debate about radio, surfaced. The magazine programme was criticised for creating a 'sort of radio pneada'. The series, *This is Northern Ireland* surely had the verb in the wrong tense. But in the middle of these Elysian memories David Bleakeley and Sam Hanna Bell rediscovered people who had been involved in the 1907 strike, when Larkin came to the Belfast docks. Their descriptions of the ruthlessness and poverty of their lives, and a country voice remembering the hedge schools, showed what good Features programmes could do. Such snippets, of course, also highlighted how seldom they were done.

Establishment values were more likely, emerging in the oddest contexts. For example, there was an uncomfortable division within Northern Ireland between those who had volunteered, or 'joined up', and those who stayed at home. It was sustained until relatively recently in the use of World War Two military titles, Captain X and Major Y. A classic example of how this manifested itself in broadcasting at the end of the war is this from 1948: 'Victor McAllister, distinguished R.A.F. pilot 1940-46, night fighter pilot in N. Africa, Sicily, and Italy; D.F.C. and Bar, D.F.M., will give a talk to farmers on 23rd February, 1948 on fertilizers and manures.'[18] With the experience gained during the war, and with the equipment available, there was effective use of the mobile recording systems, and *Provincial Journey, Up Against It* and *They do it for Love* toured successfully.

In the 1947 BBC Handbook, Louis MacNeice wrote 'Scripts Wanted'. He pleads elegantly for more writers to contribute drama and features to the third programme, which had been launched in 1946. MacNeice opened up the notion of 'authorship' – an area which continues to be of concern and is much debated by media critics today. In radio, he argued, 'The author therefore has far more say about the performance of his piece than in any other medium which involves teamwork.'[19] That control was significant in the success of the individual voices of, for example, Denis Johnston, Jack Loudan, Sam Hanna Bell and Joseph Tomelty. The close relationship between producer and writer working closely together is discernible from Tyrone Guthrie, James Mageean, Sam Denton, through to Robert Coulter.

Two years after MacNeice's call to writers, in April 1949, Northern Ireland ran a competition, '£50 for a story'. By August, 250 scripts had been received, Janet McNeill was discovered, and the judges noted a reduction in the kitchen comedy format.[20] On reflection, this welcome seems a little ironic because 1949 saw the introduction of Joe Tomelty's Belfast family, *The McCooeys* which was to command an audience of one third of the population. This weekly series was written by Tomelty and the majority of the actors came from the Belfast Group Theatre. It dealt humorously with an incident each week and James Young's portrayal of a window-cleaner brought him his first national recognition. Listening to the programme, indeed any programme, 40 years later, out of its contemporary environment, transplanted from its social context, is to exhume a skeleton for autopsy. Nonetheless, what still lives on in the twenty-minute programmes is the tight dramatic structure, and the vocal variety of J.G. Devlin. The listener was taken out of the studio to the McCooey home as the announcer introduces the

programme: 'The microphone will again be dropping in on the
family . . . the microphone will be visiting the McCooeys.' The
programme is social and broadcasting history. It attempted to
reflect attitudes using the well-tried strategy of humour – Belfast
humour which has similar safety and defence mechanisms to
humour in Liverpool or Glasgow. The father was a shipyard
worker, the son an electrician, one daughter worked in a clothes
shop, the other in an office. Even the grandfather, who had retired
from the railway, worked as a night-watchman. The mother was
'wise and uncomplaining'. It reassured post-war Belfast that nor-
mality had returned – all the men were employed. The signature
tune, *My Aunt Jane* brought a safe world with it. Grandfather sums
up the patriarchal attitude to woman in the line (when referring
to their use of make-up), 'Aping the poor uneducated savage in
cannibal land . . . all wimin down the ages have impeded the
progress of civilisation . . . paint and feathers . . . they're loath to
leave behind their inheritance from primitive humanity.'[21] The
'Grandfather' had an impeccable pedigree as a theatrical device.
Like Alf Garnett years later, he was a literary character, the fool, a
mix of registers, the writer's voice. (We should note that, on air,
the London continuity announcer in 1947, speaking with perfect
diction, could still say, 'Now what about a sample from the darky
minstrel show, *The Coloured Coons*.'

The McCooeys, the comedies of the Group Theatre, and, a few
years later, James Young's own monologues, did not attempt to
examine, nor to reflect upon, what contributed to the specific
nature of Northern Ireland, and of Belfast in particular, they
'showed' an idealised version of it. Audiences laughed both at,
and with, the characters and their dilemmas. It was the complex
reaction of an audience which was one generation away from the
world they were hearing on the radio; one remove from the
kitchens and shops they paid to see in the theatre. There was a
cathartic response by many in those audiences. They could laugh
at members of the family who had not moved into the post-war
world – people they now met only at weddings and funerals.

The popular *Dick Barton, Special Agent* (1946) was a thriller series
from London, (weekdays 6.45 p.m.) where the forces of evil were
defeated by the 'Boys Own Paper' heroes of Dick, Jock and Snowy.
What remains of interest is that its content and approach were
closely monitored. Strict guidelines to the behaviour of the characters presaged the contemporary watershed strictures to be

found in the ITC and BBC guides to good taste and decency. 'Barton's violence is restricted to clean socks on the jaw. The refinements of unarmed combat taught to British Commandos cannot be practised by him or his colleagues. (The war was less that two years before.) When involved in a brawl he must be equally matched or outnumbered.Sex plays no part in the Barton adventures. He can have no flirtations or affairs and his enemies must have no molls or mistresses. Swearing and bad language generally cannot be used by any character.'[22] And despite all these guidelines being adhered to, the programme was still the subject of a paper in 1950, '*Dick Barton* and juvenile delinquency.'[23]

When *Blackboard Jungle* (1955), featuring Bill Haley's *Rock around the Clock*, was screened in local cinemas, the nation found itself under attack by a power as threatening as the Axis forces. Even outrage at giving the GAA results on the Sabbath paled in comparison to this cultural Blitzkrieg. It was resisted on *Any Questions* by such pillars of moral rectitude as Jeremy Thorpe, 'Jazz comes from the jungle. This is jungle music taken to its logical conclusion. This is musical Mau Mau.' and by Lord Boothby who was, 'Seeking to protect the youth of the country.'[24] The BBC's Dance Music Policy Committee acted equally responsibly on behalf of the youth of the early 1950's by banning such songs as 'A corset can do a lot for a lady' and 'Has anyone seen my pom'.

Radio and television, continued to bring live events into homes in Northern Ireland. The Coronation created a major demand for television, but the flickering black and white screens did not bring live pictures of the State Visit of the Queen to Northern Ireland in June 1953. 'Under the present limitations of the temporary Television Service in Northern Ireland it is not possible to transmit direct TV broadcasts.'[25] The visit was filmed for *Television Newsreel* and live commentary went out on radio – Richard Dimbleby at Stormont and Geoffrey Talbot at Hillsborough – but the local man, John Body, was left outside to report on the Garden Party. A month later the 'Twelfth' was recorded and presented at 7.45 p.m. because, 'Loyalty to the crown is, of course, one of the first principles of the Orange Order'. During the 1950s, among the sports broadcasts were, The Ulster Grand Prix, rugby internationals, cricket and a little soccer, implicitly demonstrating that religio-class preferences had changed little from the pre-war years.

The alliance of the BBC's metropolitan influences and its Protestant cultural values continued to dominate broadcasting in

Northern Ireland until the Independent Television Authority franchised regional television. Its emphasis on regional autonomy in local programming coincided with the beginning of a challenge to radio's supremacy which had come ironically with the televising of the Coronation. The first BBC TV studio was commissioned in February, 1959, just eight months before UTV's studios at Havelock House challenged the BBC's thirty-five year monopoly of local broadcasting. A superficially similar coincidence occurred when BBC Radio Ulster went on the air in 1975, a few months before Downtown was awarded the Independent Local Radio franchise.

It would be easy to dismiss the introduction of Radio Ulster as a natural, defensive tactic, a pre-emptive strike. But that would be too simplistic. It would both distort the evidence and ignore the significance for the whole of Northern Ireland, of the momentous events experienced since 1968.

In 1972 BBC NI collated statistics in preparation for its submission to the BBC Committee on Broadcasting Coverage. In the very full discussion document *The BBC in Northern Ireland*, BBC Memorandum No 3, it was pointed out that: 'It is a major weakness in Northern Ireland's radio service that the morning current affairs programme has to be limited to 15 mins. . . . an increase from 15 to 25 mins a day would meet a real community need.'[26] The total number of broadcast hours in radio per annum was 638, an average output of fewer than two hours per day. 400 of those hours were not news programmes. It is difficult to equate that fact against the mayhem and political instability of the early 1970s. However, the memorandum endorses the thesis that this short paper has argued, '. . . there is no disguising the fact that the service is substantially provided <u>by</u> the Network and <u>for</u> the Network audience.' (Underlining as in the memo.) The substantive issue of giving the region more opportunity to opt-out is raised in the memo (Section 2, paragraph 6), 'One solution, probably the most effective, would be for Northern Ireland to alter the form of its present output to provide a service more in line with that given by local radio stations – say a 'Radio "Ulster" for the whole community.' Significantly, it develops the notion to include 'suitable inject-points' and mentions, Belfast, Newry, and Londonderry. The present pattern of local studios is sketched out – so, too is the crucial need for development of the transmitter network if there were to be real audience choice.

In February, 1974, the Controller, Northern Ireland, Richard

Francis sent a Memorandum to Head of Television and to Head of Radio.[27] This was a clear report on the state of play comparing the resources available within the BBC in Northern Ireland with those of Wales and Scotland. He concludes, 'I am convinced that these statements are realistic and that the Region is short of revenue to an alarming degree. We cannot continue to run BBC Northern Ireland on a war footing, requiring staff permanently to work excessive overtime and producers to work in sensitive areas on shoestring budgets.' (p.2) The Controller set out a budget proposal, and the number of Engineering and Production posts he estimated that would be required to maintain an output of an adequate standard, without the demands of expansion. He concluded, 'There can be little doubt about the part which the BBC could play in helping to heal this troubled community in the years ahead.' (p2) There was an air of optimism in the Spring air. While the Loyalists refused to recognise the Assembly, bombings in Londonderry had been reduced from 59 in June, to 9 in December, 1973. There is no indication of what was to follow for a further 21 years, as he concluded, 'It's no bad thing that Northern Ireland is no longer headline news, but it is unthinkable that it should revert to being a backwater of the BBC.'

The response from London was properly contextualised with reference to the ongoing revisions of wavelengths that were under discussion by the Crawford Committee. Pressure for the introduction of the new service was 'specifically supported by Sir Stewart Crawford himself and by other members of the Committee'.[28] It noted that, 'All these promptings preceded the recent crisis.' However, the memorandum recognised that a serious escalation of tension had occurred, 'it is our understanding that the U.W.C. strike is felt to have made the need for early action even more urgent.' The place of Radio 4 in the output was explicitly accepted; as was the need to have two wavelengths. 'It is argued that this would give the Province a good regional service which might make some contribution as a unifying force, but at the same time an undiluted Radio 4 might provide a strengthening sense of membership of the United Kingdom.' Civil unrest and vicious urban and rural violence had been part of the daily life of Northern Ireland by this stage. London's hope that 'undiluted Radio 4' would promote a sense of membership suggests that the aims and actions of certain groups within Northern Ireland did not make a deep impression in some quarters in London! It was recognised that there was a need for urgent action. However, less than half the money that Richard Francis had requested in order to maintain standards, was on offer to set up Radio Ulster. In his introduction to the feasibility paper, *Radio Ulster Discussion Paper*, the Controller recognised the significance of the extra radio programming initiated during the U.W.C. strike, 'We believe some of the impetus of the extra programming during the U.W.C. strike should be harnessed in anticipation of an early launching of Radio Ulster.'[29]

The UWC Strike had alarmed Northern Ireland people, especially in Belfast and the larger towns. The importance of accurate and frequent information had become an essential drip feed to an ill patient. Not only did people want to know what had been and was happening, but they needed to know that in their locality, or on their routes home, nothing was happening. Before Radio Ulster opened, it had been accepted in Northern Ireland that it would be an opt-out station based upon a mix of BBC Radios 1,2,3, and 4. Richard Francis consistently underlined, in detail, the inadequate resources; the lack of proper transmission wavelengths; and he foresaw 'severe problems in providing studio and office accommodation'.

On the 30 July 1974 the D.G. approved a BBC Note to the Crawford Committee approving the new radio service, BBC Radio Ulster. It recorded that, 'The name "BBC Radio Ulster" has been accepted by the Northern Ireland Advisory Council. When members considered alternatives, they found "Radio 6" pejorative and "Radio Northern Ireland" too clumsy.'[30]

Radio Ulster went on air on 1 January 1975 on 224m, which had been the Radio 4 wavelength. It did not, at first, cover the whole of Northern Ireland, never mind the nine counties that constitute Ulster. The geographical areas covered by the two Radio 4 transmitters, one at Derry and one on Divis, did not meet and therefore, did not serve the middle; nor did they reach the Glens of Antrim. Being a medium wave frequency, continental competition made receiving its evening and late night programmes a hit and miss affair. Despite Dick Francis' repeated requests at the highest level, for proper resourcing, it had been poorly provided for. It had a small news room and some music and drama production. Actual local output increased by very little. Significantly, the piecemeal opt-out did have benefits in loosening up Sunday from the Radio 4 schedule.

One of the achievments of BBC radio in Northern Ireland over the years has been the consistent quality of the output from Educational Broadcasting. During my time with the Advisory Committee and the SBC NI, the list of contributors resembled a roll-call of Irish writers: Heaney, Muldoon, Mahon; its staff from James Hawthorne to Pat Loughrey have demonstrated a commitment to quality programmes. Debates about regional autonomy, the use of the Irish language, administrative interference and creativity and interpretations of Irish history were the stuff of committee meetings then. Radio Drama, too, requires a special section to record its long history. It might be called 'Astonish me tomorrow.'[31]

In 1977, a new Assistant Head of Programmes was appointed. Don Anderson, a former BBC reporter, had proven success with the Downtown Radio team. It had broadcast music and news to the local community in the vernacular and had abolished the traditional, formal script; the personnel were 'multi-skilled'; they had no long-established codes of practice or strongly-defended demarcation lines; not was there an intimidating engineering tradition. It had been a very different climate from that at the BBC and Anderson was to bring this style to Ormeau Avenue. In order to establish a particular identity to BBC Radio Ulster, the first aim, for Anderson, was to try to make it cohere, to appear to be less 'like a gruyere cheese' of broadcasting.[32] Due to the limited resources available, documentary, drama and journalism could not be increased. The pattern for peak radio listening was 'drive-time', mid-morning programmes and the evening roundup between 5 and 6 pm. To exploit that pattern, the mid-morning was given over to 2 hours of Gloria Hunniford.

But such a change re-energised the consistent debate about the role of local BBC broadcasting and the accusation that it was a poor substitute for Radio 4. Where there was no wavelength choice, the audience, largely middle-class and Protestant, wanted the provincial choice of the metropolitan output, rather than the parochial local product. But the hostile reaction to local programmes filling the afternoon slots of *Women's Hour* and the *Afternoon Play* came not only from the listeners. The former Head of Programmes at Ormeau Avenue, Ronald Mason, had been appointed Head of BBC Radio Drama in London. His displeasure at his listeners hearing the London stereo output on a mono channel was forcibly expressed in a brief telephone call to the Controller of Radio Ulster.

The special place of organised religion in Northern Ireland is known internationally. Indeed, the first experimental broadcast on the Belfast station, 2BE, took place on 15 September 1924 and the first meeting of the Religious Advisory Committee was 3 November![33] It is hardly a surprise that when Radio 4's *Morning Service* was appropriated by a religious service from Northern Ireland that the Controller of Radio Ulster was called the 'anti-Christ'. Appropriating Radio 4's Sunday schedule was, however, an important statement that Radio Ulster had the nerve to establish a regional identity. While such a move was unpopular with its middle-class audience, it was crucial in giving the new station autonomy and credibility. Without that resilience and commitment, the potential too become an opt-in station would have been squandered. The talk-based radio that we have available now was hard won.

But such a comparatively 'commercial', informal approach had its critics within the organisation. The pressure for the newsroom to handle a large number of stories, to select, edit, script and package them, often when a bulletin was on air, meant that a change in professional practice was necessary. The reporter and the producer wanted to edit or dub the sound tape themselves. This need for immediate action, omitting the trained editor, brought them into conflict with the BBC Audio Unit. Editors had a special place in the production of quality broadcasts in radio and television and their contribution to drama, features, and music programmes was comparable to that of the writers, composers or producers. But they resisted the new approaches that technological and production changes were demanding (for example, the 'producer's edit' was continued). The birth of what is now termed 'multi-skilling' was not an easy one.

The commissioning of Radio Foyle in September 1979, completed the movement from metropolitan Imperialism to local involvement. In terms of commercial stations, its structure and approach was a commonplace but within the BBC tradition, local radio was anarchy. But the loosening up of the usual organisation of radio to enable local stations to come on air must be acknowledged. The debates of the 1980s around 'Journalistic Ethics' (*The Listener*, January, 1981) which discussed the notion of the journalist as citizen, were displaced by those which discussed the broadcaster as citizen. Radio Foyle, like the airwaves, became more accessible to the public; the vernacular was the accepted speech

style; programmes came from self-op studios, without the supervi-
sion of Audio Unit personnel; efficient working practices were
positively sought after; it broadcast to both the *Londonderry Sentinel*
and to the *Derry Journal* reader. It caused some irritation at
Ormeau Avenue because Foyle was opt-outing from the Region. It
did not confuse relating to the community with attempting to heal
its wounds. Like Radio Ulster, its programmes, too, made a statement. By reporting the business of Derry City council, Radio Foyle
affirmed that the old pre-1968 order had changed radically: middle-class Protestant dominance had gone.

Programme content today suggests that the centre seems to
have become more remote, but each evening at six o'clock on
Radio Ulster, Big Ben strikes and provides a reminder that local
independence remains fragile and vulnerable. However, the frag-
mentation bomb of cable is fused and waiting with 100 audio
channels available. The process of democratisation is ready to shift
into another gear.

NOTES

1. *The Observer*, 2 April 1995.
2. *BBC Year Book*, 1947, p.39.
3. *Pure Radio*, BBC 1, 3 November 1977 (Tape BA34).
4. ibid.
5. A. Heuser, Paper to the Annual Louis MacNeice Symposium, University of Ulster, September 1994.
6. J. Stallworthy, *Louis MacNeice* (London: Faber and Faber, 1995), p.444.
7. *Pure Radio*.
8. K. Ward, *Mass Communications and the Modern World*, (London: Macmillan, 1989). p.125.
9. *The Friend in the Corner* 1936, Radio 4, 1 December 1992.
10. ibid.
11. *Pure Radio*.
12. D. Cranston, 'A Look Back', in P. Lindsay (ed.) *Media and Modern Society in Ireland*, (Dublin: Social Studies Conference, 1993) p.10.
13. 'BBC in Northern Ireland', *BBC Handbook* 1949.
14. R. Cathcart, *The Most Contrary Region*, (Belfast: Blackstaff Press, 1984).
15. *70 Years of the BBC*, Radio Ulster, programme 1.
16. *'BBC in Northern Ireland'*.
17. *An Echo of Voices*, tx. 16 September 1974 (Index BBC Archive, Folk and Transport Museum, Mus. 99).
18. *Northern Ireland Broadcasting News*, vol.14, 1948.
19. *BBC Handbook* 1947.
20. *Northern Ireland Broadcasting News*, vol. 6 1949 and vol. 35 1949.
21. *The McCooeys* Prog.176. (Mus 669).
22. *Friend in the Corner* 1947.

23. 'Dick Barton and Juvenile Delinquency: A Listener Research Paper', 15 May 1950, quoted by Asa Briggs, *The History of Broadcasting in the United Kingdom, Vol. iv: Sound and Vision (Oxford: Oxford University Press, 1979). p.58.*

24. *Friend in the Corner* 1947.

25. *Northern Ireland Broadcasting News,* vol. 27 1953.

26. 'Committee on Broadcasting Coverage' *BBC Memorandum No 3. The BBC in Northern Ireland. A memorandum on behalf of the Northern Ireland Advisory Council, August 1973*

27. Memorandum, *Maintenance of Northern Ireland Output.* From Controller Northern Ireland to Managing Director Television and Managing Director Radio 5 February 1974.

28. Letter from Managing Director, Radio (Ian Trethowan) to Under Secretary, Broadcasting Department (Jolyon Dromogoole, Esq.), Home Office at Waterloo Bridge House, London. SE1 8UA. 20 June 1974.

29. Memorandum, *Maintenance of Northern Ireland Output.*

30. A BBC note for the Crawford Committee, *BBC Radio Ulster* B.M. (74) 92 D.P 30.7.74 (Caversham).

31. Dan Gilbert, personal interview. (The quote is Tyrone Guthrie's exit line from rehearsals.)

32. Personal Interview with Don Anderson, ITC Officer for Northern Ireland, March 1995.

33. BBC in Northern Ireland, 1949.

ACKNOWLEDGEMENTS.

Particular thanks for their time and assistance to Pat Loughrey, Rosemary Kelly, Don Anderson, Jackie Kavanagh at the BBC Written Archives Centre at Caversham, Grainne Loughran and the staff at the BBC Sound Archives at Cultra, Co. Down.

My special thanks to the late Dan Gilbert for generously opening his library to me during the preparation of this chapter and for all his encouragement and support for the Media Studies degree at Coleraine since 1978.

ABOVE SUSPICION OR CONTROVERSY? : THE DEVELOPMENT OF THE BBC'S IRISH HISTORY PROGRAMME FOR SCHOOLS IN NORTHERN IRELAND.

A Personal Recollection

James Hawthorne

Any account of BBC programmes on Irish history, like the history itself, poses the problem of where to begin.

One must go back long before the first programme was ever made and before my own recruitment to BBC Northern Ireland in July 1960 as the region's first specialist schools producer. At that point I was a teacher of nine years experience – with only about thirty-four to go. Attracted by an advertisement which specifically asked for teacher-applicants, I joined a swarm of asylum seekers and somehow managed to swim to the farther shore that bit faster than all the others.

I was soon to discover that the thrust to produce schools broadcasts from Belfast had by no means come from there; nor from London; but from Newcastle-upon-Tyne! In defiance of geography, Tyneside had been joined to Northern Ireland by BBC Engineering – we had long shared the same Home Service wavelength. The rather perverse view was that, as Northern Ireland was a small area and that within that area few schools were using BBC radio or television broadcasts, there was no case for a full-time education officer based in Belfast to drum up interest. The task could easily be added to the duties of the education officer in Newcastle-upon-Tyne who covered the north-east of England! The effect was that Northern Ireland lagged further and further behind other regions. As to actually producing its own broadcasts, the BBC management in Belfast had consistently expressed its misgivings about being able to meet the quality standards set by London, about having sufficient material to complement local studies and, above all, about the problems inherent in the separation of Catholic and Protestant schools; in short, a deep fear of stirring up controversies, educational and political.

Things changed dramatically, however, when in 1960, a certain Mr Leslie Davidson became the north-east of England education officer, a remarkable enthusiast who revelled in the Irish side of his duties. From his Tyneside office his vicarious ambition took the form of a campaign for Northern Ireland schools to use more of the BBC's output and he even dared to advocate a production facility in Belfast to provide more localised subject matter. Scotland and Wales had been producing programmes for their own areas for several years.[1] Davidson was not deterred by Belfast's resistance. He had managed to have the region represented on the Schools Broadcasting Council in London and he then created a subcommittee in Belfast in pursuance of his cause. In its chairman, the progressive and influential Dr. Hawnt, Director of Education for Belfast, he found a staunch and effective ally. And thus the regional management of the BBC was finally dragooned into a new radio production venture; an outcome unlikely to make things easy for that teacher-recruit who was to deliver the programmes. And there was another factor.

BBC *Children's Hour* had run its course and there was much professional ill-feeling about its demise and, understandably, about embarking on something new and vaguely similiar. From the very early days of programme-making in the region, Cicely Mathews – a household name – had been the producer of *Children's Hour* broadcasts and now she was virtually redundant. Those who had written for her were short of work. An outsider was now appointed and the word was that few of the old *Children's Hour* team would have a role in developing specialised programmes for schools.

If BBC Belfast was finding it difficult to overcome its self-doubt it is only fair to add that its new-found courage was being undermined by serious doubts within the local educational establishment. Could the region match those 'beautiful', well-elocuted programmes from London, already much admired by Northern Ireland teachers? Setting controversy aside, attempting to serve both value systems, Protestant and Catholic, might prove impossible.

Within two months of my notice to my previous employer still to run, and innocent of Olympian struggles within and without the BBC, I happened to telephone the Assistant Head of Programmes[2] in Belfast with a specific request. I had been invited to appear on Ulster Television, as one-quarter of a singing group. I felt I should put by new BBC boss in the picture. As he was in fact a Presbyterian clergyman I should not have been too surprised when he intoned a verse from First Corinthians: 'All things are lawful unto me but all things are not expedient'. Not daring to be inexpedient I was obliged to turn down UTV's *Teatime with Tommy*.

From that point onwards, and months into my early BBC career, I seemed to be engulfed by inexpediency, trapped in a safe defensive scheme which the region had already worked out. Addressed invariably by my surname, I was reminded that I was only on probation, that the project had been forced upon the region against its seasoned judgement, that I should not use my title 'producer' until I had actually produced something, that I should work both to the Assistant Head of Programmes and to Cicely Matthews and attach myself – if they would take me – to local producers to learn the ropes. A number of programme subjects had actually been mandated and there was an arrangement, already paid for out of my budget, with Queen's University's Geography department for consultation and scripts.

In reality however I was the property of a London department and I had to follow its rigorous planning schedules and the deadlines set by the Schools Broadcasting Council. The Council was a majestic invention, chaired by Sir Charles Morris, dating almost from the days of the BBC's founding father, Lord Reith, it had been set up to guide BBC's highly prized programmes for schools. It presided over a number of high-powered committees and it had its own staff of Education Officers in regional offices all over Britain, of whom Leslie Davidson in Newcastle-upon-Tyne was one. It was the Council, not the programme departments of BBC Education, which theoretically assessed educational needs and drew up what were called 'commissions' for programme series. The BBC, resources permitting, would then respond with proposals for actual programmes for the Councils' consideration. In regional terms, an important formality was that the programmes would be submitted, not by the Region, but by the Head of Educational Broadcasting in London[3]. Before programmes could go ahead, the relevant expert committee – with the BBC and the Council officials merely 'in attendance' – would first have to express the momentous view that the proposals 'conformed to the commission'.

Far from being an arcane and bureaucratic procedure, this method of developing new series ensured that BBC educational broadcasting had a clear and stable direction and purpose. Within that formal division of responsibility however, educational policy makers and educational producers could work closely. Short of allies, Davidson and I kept in close touch and we had strong support from Schools Broadcasting's management in London, notably the inspiring Norman Lloyd Williams and his deputy Ivan Gilman[4]. Our common resolve was that the new schools programmes from Belfast should on no account be a revamped version of the Children's Hour programmes which had gone before. The audience would be a new one, not the intelligent cream of the mainly middle class who had turned to the wireless out of interest – and who had now defected to television. The schools audience would be ordinary children in ordinary schools taught by ordinary teachers and the programmes would be taken in an ordinary classroom setting.

There was another compelling reason why Davidson and I had to get together. On my very first BBC day – the morning spent in a tiny phone-less and furniture-less office – we were to attend a crucial meeting and outline plans for the new programmes. The Council had already identified an age group and described a general educational need. Davidson and I added the final touches to a suitable 'commission' and came up with a series title, *Today and Yesterday* – to which the words 'for Northern Ireland' were added by local management on 'policy grounds', lest Geordie classrooms might presume too much.

The Commission was to provide a broadcast series:

for children of 10-13 in Primary and Secondary schools bearing in mind the needs of wide age range classes such as are found in many country schools; which shall widen children's interests, knowledge and experience of Northern Ireland and its affairs past and present and make them more curious about their own country. . . which shall act as a starting point for further exploration by teachers and children, offering opportunities for varied and enterprising follow-up work; which shall draw on a wide range of material, and more particularly relevant to social history, geography, industry, agriculture and topics of current interest; in the main. . . non fictional but literary topics are not excluded; which shall be accompanied by teachers' notes explaining the aims of the series and containing suggestions for handling and following up the broadcasts and by an illustrated pupils' pamphlet. . . .[5]

On 22 November 1960, three bewildering weeks into my BBC career, the commission was duly adopted and then I had to describe in speculative detail my proposals for the first ten programmes to begin in April. Meanwhile I had to start on a thirty-two page fully-illustrated book to accompany the series and a set of notes and ideas for teachers to meet urgent printers' deadlines months before the first programme would be recorded. Within a further few short weeks I had to commit the BBC to a second series of thirty-two detailed programme ideas for inclusion in the Annual Programme for 1961-62 which had to be notified to schools early in February – again, before a single trial programme could be made. Untrained, under pressure from regional management and committed to a total of forty-two programmes which I had no real idea how to make, I wondered whether that metaphorical swim to freedom had been worth it.

At a meeting of the Council's Northern Ireland subcommittee on 22 February 1961, a classic 'policy problem' raised its inevitable head. Within a group of topics about 'Buying and Selling' I had proposed three rather functional programmes about the marketing of cattle, eggs and potatoes and a fourth entitled 'Our Coal Supplies'. The Assistant Head of Programmes got wind of the coal idea and immediately banned it! Hidden in that deceptively innocuous topic, there were, apparently, levels of political chicanery of which my untutored mind was naively unaware! Was this to be one of the great controversies long feared by regional management? So serious were the problems in the Assistant Head's mind, that he was not prepared to reveal the full reasons for his objections and thus, to this day, I am unaware of what grave difficulties a programme about coal in Northern Ireland might have caused my illustrious employer.

It was time to play the London card and I engineered that 'proposals from the Controller of Educational Broadcasting' should include the condemned topic. Dr. Hawnt was at his disingenuous best and asked the hapless Assistant Head to explain his difficulty. The Council listened in bemused silence. The result was inevitable and proved to be a turning point for future programme development. Sensing the difficult atmosphere in Belfast, London had brought me over for production training and experience. In London I was dropped in at the deep end and found myself producing network programmes dealing with current affairs – my inaugural effort was about a deteriorating situation in Indo-China! The first-ever Northern Ireland schools' pamphlets and notes then appeared from the printers and were warmly approved by the cognoscenti. I returned to Belfast slightly more confident to take on the task ahead.

Magnanimous in victory, Davidson recorded the Great Coal Debate in a low-key minute:

> Some doubts were expressed. . . about the educational value of a unit on Buying and Selling. . . but it was finally agreed that the successful treatment of this unit was a matter which could be left to the Producer.[6]

Thirty-four years on (1995), *Today and Yesterday* is still broadcast, although its commission has long since been modified as overall output has expanded. Over the years its producers have included notable broadcasting 'names' – David Hammond and Tony McAuley and the present BBC Controller, Patrick Loughrey. A short-list drawn from its many distinguished contributors would include Seamus Heaney, Brian Friel, Bernard McLaverty, John McGahern, William Conor, Sean O'Boyle, Patrick Boyle, Sam Hanna Bell, JJ Campbell, Maurice Leitch, James Plunkett, ATQ Stewart, Michael J Murphy, Stewart Parker, Stewart Love, Rosemary Sutcliffe, Michael Longley. . . In its early pioneering days Norman Harrison was the series' most innovative and prolific script-writer. In 1965 we got our first Education Officer, Tony Fleck, who later became the IBA's Regional Officer.

An important function of the Schools Broadcasting Council was to conduct research and to produce critical reports of programmes to test their effectiveness in terms of the agreed 'commission'. Thus, from the very beginning of *Today and Yesterday*, we had a panel of user-schools who sent in weekly comments under precise criteria. Reports were also written by the Education Officer and, from time to time, there would be special reviews. The system was a recipe for friction between producer and assessor but the Northern Ireland set-up was singularly free of such problems and producers often visited classrooms themselves while their broadcasts were being transmitted.

The new schools broadcasts were by no means universally successful, although it must be said that part of the problem lay with
stern classroom traditions, if not with some teachers – there had
been practically no classroom teaching of local geography or history to prepare the broadcasting ground. The material from the
BBC was not only new to children, it was new to teachers as well
and often there were expectations which no twenty-minute radio
programme could ever meet. Evidence of this came out in critical
comments. I recall a rather moving and beautiful programme
about Dunluce Castle which echoed the wave-swept coast of North
Antrim and told of a tragic love-pact. I was in an East Belfast classroom during its transmission and both children and teacher were
enthralled. But in Leslie Davidson's collation of the panel reports
he wrote:

> This programme was not received with the same enthusiasm as
> some of the others. . . perhaps this was because it was historical
> rather than geographical. According to one teacher: it would
> really have taken four broadcasts to cover the subject ade-
> quately. . . the children were quite prepared to accept the
> unusual aspects of the subject such as Sorley Boy, ghosts and the
> falling of the kitchen into the sea. . . they were more interested
> in these side issues than in the education aim of the pro-
> gramme. . . disappointment was caused by not saying enough
> about the tunnel, failing to explain why certain events hap-
> pened, failing to describe the interior of the castle, not men-
> tioning the methods of construction. . . .[6]

Ulster teachers wanted value.

It would however be wrong to conclude that panel reports presented only an uneven and unreliable picture, though of the same
broadcast one teacher could write:

> Over simplified, narrow in scope and commonplace in subject;

While another wrote:

> There was no need for me to question these children on the
> subject matter. They wanted to talk and to compare the activi-
> ties and hardships of the family with their own homes.[7]

Collectively, teachers' reports were establishing a need to split the series into two, one for primary and one for secondary children and there was growing evidence that history themes, well-written, were working well and that there was a capacity for the 'real' history that lay hidden under a notorious self-imposed security blanket. Various *Today and Yesterday* successes pointed the way. Individual programmes on Carrickfergus, Moneymore and Armagh touched on the conflict between Planter and Gael while a four-part unit on the rise of Belfast in the 1963 Spring term and a stylish six-part 'Queen Elizabeth and the O'Neils' the following year (script by Jo Manton, special music composed by Havelock Nelson) were demonstrating that full-blooded Irish History could be the next major step if a separate secondary series were to be developed.

In its research report, the Council stated:

There is no doubt that these programmes gave children an unusually vivid picture of this period in Irish history. This was because of the extremely successful dramatisations. The quality of the writing was consistently high, the use of harp, trumpet and song to create atmosphere, to indicate a change of scene, or to establish location was very successful. The atmosphere of restlessness and instability in Ireland during this period, the portrayal of the Irish peasantry, the impressions of the O'Neils, the romance and tragedy – all these were excellently realised, giving a very full and accurate picture of Elizabethan Ireland.

Of great importance too is the reaction of teachers and children to the presentation of Irish history as a subject. The fact that this group of programmes received such high approbation is in itself an indication that such programmes are welcome, and further, that given impartiality, there is little objection among reporting schools to the presentation of Irish history.[8]

We were also conducting more formal research with curriculum experts and with 'the Ministry' and, as might be expected, there was much bemoaning that Irish history was not taught, many theories as to why and no clear idea how it should be approached. The value of social history was broadly recognised but somebody had to break the taboo of political history if social history were to be understood. Among a welter of SBC reports between 1962 and 1964 one simple sentence stands out:

The teaching of Irish History in Northern Ireland presents especial problems![9]

And yet another glimpse into the obvious:

The main difficulty in broadcasting Irish history is of course political.[10]

There was one other factor. Independent of all our research, I was personally convinced that Irish history was of overwhelming importance and, in an entirely egocentric way, I simply wanted to break new ground. BBC Education in London had always been supportive, but this time round a little more reassurance was required – there is always a point when English administrations find the going in Ireland too dangerous! Yet when things eventually move in the higher echelons of BBC policy-making, they can do so with surprising speed. A hint was dropped that money might be made available for an additional term of secondary programmes and, before the ink was dry on the last piece of research, I had to put together a set of proposals for an actual series in time for the meeting of the SBC on 5 May 1964. Once again, a commission was essential and this was worked out jointly with Leslie Davidson. It called for a series of weekly broadcasts for one term:

for children of 14 and 15 in Secondary schools. . . which shall present Irish history principally of the nineteenth and twentieth centuries in its own right and not merely as an adjunct to English history. . . which shall in its total impact seek to make clearer the events leading to the creation of Northern Ireland, and shall provide a basis for teaching the subject so that teachers, especially in schools where the subject has not hitherto been taught at all, will be encouraged to develop further this field of study. . . which, recognising the strength of personal feeling in this field, shall take particular care to be fair and accurate, but shall not avoid controversial issues. . . which shall be accompanied by Teachers' notes containing details of each broadcast and any necessary background to the topic, and by a Pupils' Pamphlet described as essential. . .[11]

This was it!

The title *Two Centuries of Irish History* seemed to invent itself but, in the light of earlier experience, I kept it to myself. I proposed topics about the United Irishmen, the Famine, the Fenians and Sinn Féin, the Unionists, the Home Rule crisis, the Easter Rising, the Civil War and the Troubles. I though such topics might give an early signal that punches were unlikely to be pulled!

I presented my ideas to an incredulous SBC subcommittee. We were, after all, turning the immaculate system on its head. This time it was not the Council identifying the educational need and telling the BBC what should be done, but an unusually passionate BBC attempting to win over the Council. Opinions were naturally divided about going ahead and there was a rearguard action from a senior Ministry Inspector who argued that we should put the emphasis on social history. As luck would have it, I was to run a playback of a *Today and Yesterday* programme at the meeting and I had chosen 'The Battle of the Yellow Ford', a positively heart-warming story of how the O'Neils, the O'Donnells, the MacDonnells and the Maguires had routed an invading English army in 1598. That helped. The minutes record that it was:

> an excellent and encouraging example of the kind of imaginative contribution Radio could make for schools wishing to take Irish history.[12]

By the end of the meeting Dr. Hawnt had got his last sheep safely into the pen. The decision was clear; there would be a new 'experimental' Irish history series in January 1965.

Because of increasing pressure – I had also been providing Mathematics publications and programmes for the National Home Service Network – a BBC expert assessor of 'workloads' had pronounced that my output was the equivalent of one-and-a-half persons! Even BBC administration might have found it taxing to recruit half a newcomer but the upshot, in anticipation of expansion, was to appoint David Hammond who had already been writing imaginatively for *Today and Yesterday*. David would take over much of the programme and support me with the new series but very soon David's talents were also being siphoned off for Network to create a special series for what were at that time euphemistically called 'less able children'. Each of our Network series was to run for several years, the first-ever to be produced by a region.[13]

The final titles for *Two Centuries of Irish History* were as follows:

Big House and Mud Cabin (Ireland in the late eighteenth
  century)
The United Irishmen
Daniel O'Connell
The Famine
Industrial Revolution
Parnell and Gladstone
Fenian and Sinn Féin
Ulster Will Fight
The Easter Rising
The Troubles
Northern Ireland'

Six writers[14], with a combination of experience in radio and teaching, wrote the scripts and I managed to secure three distinguished consultants; Professors JC Beckett of Queen's , WL McCracken of Magee College and GA Hayes-McCoy of Galway University who also wrote two scripts. If we were to broadcast Irish history it would have to be done well or not at all.

I had been determined that the advent of Irish history from BBC Northern Ireland should be a very public event. It must be remembered that this was long before the days of Radio Ulster and, needless to say, before commercial competition. Northern Ireland programmes were opt-outs from the Home Service. Schools programmes appeared within the normal schedules and were heard – or overheard – by listeners of all ages. Grasping the opportunity, I made sure that I did a piece on *Programme Parade* every morning a broadcast went out during school hours. 'Today's programme is about the Fenians. . .' was a new signal from Broadcasting House! Many citizens, who would later recall the series with some affection, *imagined* that they had actually heard the programmes when in fact it was only the 'trails' for peak morning audiences!

It would be wrong to suppose that *Two Centuries* was a total success but it hit the headlines – literally – 'Revolution in Radio', 'Radio History', 'New light on Ireland' and one correspondent wrote:

If the meeting [the historic meeting between Mr O'Neill and Mr Lemass] was the beginning of a great advance in economic relations in Ireland, the BBC's new history series for schools is an equally great advance in education[15].

The interim assessment of the Education Officer (25 May 1965) set out some of the strengths and shortcomings.

Special mention must first be made of the enthusiasms with which this series has been received. . .. All have praised the initiative.. in broadcasting a history series which broke new ground. . . and there is evidence that some schools using the series were introducing their children to Irish history for the first time. . . It has to be admitted that there are two views on Irish history. . . and it is gratifying that reports praise the impartiality of presentation, so that the main object has been achieved and an admirable balance, satisfactory to both parties, has been maintained. . . the success of the series has been outstanding. . .. in the eyes of teachers an educational landmark. More than one teacher at the end of the series said; the children were grateful for such a vivid picture of Irish history; and another said: we have waited twenty-five years for something like this.[16]

But there were difficulties:

. . . it has proved virtually impossible to compress two centuries. . . into eleven programmes. The result. . . has been to place considerable strain on teachers in terms of preparation and follow-up. . . and even the more academic sections. . . have been at times taxed to the utmost. It is in this sense that the programmes have perhaps not made the broad imaginative and dramatic impact which, for example, 'The O'Neils' in 'Today and Yesterday' achieved. The programmes relied successfully on the presentation of historical documents and speeches of the period. This gave the programmes more authenticity and on the whole was more suited to the age range. . . the result in part of necessity because of shortage of time and in part because of the need for maintaining the middle of the road. . . A technique used in the programmes and highly praised. . . was the use of folksongs of the period as a means of reflecting the true feelings of the people at moments of political and religious crisis. . . the effect of these songs. . . was extremely moving.

The series was repeated in Autumn 1965 with some amendments and with the addition of a revision programme. But the essential problem of compressing so much into ten or eleven broadcasts had to be addressed and preliminary work soon began on a brand new series for Autumn 1966. Entitled simply 'Irish History', topics were rearranged, there were new titles and, as a teaching aid, effectiveness was greatly improved. Some new writers were brought in. But before that could happen, the BBC Controller Robert McCall had asked that I create a book based on the existing scripts and I had to complete the task early in 1966. I was to regret that it was not the thoroughly revised Autumn 1966 programme series which we were committing to posterity.

If the BBC's management in Belfast had been unduly resistant at the beginning of schools broadcasting, one could not have faulted its support and encouragement in the years that were to follow. In Northern Ireland it is the unknown that we seem to fear most. The department developed rapidly. New series for secondary levels were started and I was working on the region's first television series for schools *Ulster in Focus* which was later taken to award-winning heights by David Hammond and which, in younger hands, is still going strong to this day.

Through the 1970s and into the 1980s, history programmes on radio – and on television – were further developed within new structures and under new headings. As the audience became more receptive and, by some mysterious process of evolution, more sophisticated, so the output increased in sophistication also. In 1978, when I returned to the BBC as Controller,[17] I wondered if our history programmes on radio may have become too eclectic; individual topics were valuable, but could a basic 'course' have been more useful. But it was no longer my responsibility – or even my privilege – to identify educational needs! That I had to leave to the Schools Broadcasting Council for Northern Ireland[18] and to the producers themselves. History, in various forms and at various levels, is still a part of the current schools department output. I continue to marvel at its excellence.

Did the BBC's Irish history efforts do anything to change the hearts and minds of young people in Northern Ireland? I recall ruefully that the last programme I personally wrote and narrated marked the beginning of our twenty-five years of violence. As a group of producers with teaching backgrounds, we were conscious of the diversity of our audiences and of the responsibility and privilege that went, as it were, with the job. Our method of developing our regional output forced us to look at fundamentals and priorities. Experience – if not plain common sense – led us beyond the formalities and limitations of the classroom. Education for Mutual Understanding and Cultural Heritage are the shiny new pillars of current school curricula. Was it we who might have laid some of the foundations?

As far back as 1970, the noted educationalist and historian Jack Magee wrote:

> There has been a good deal of talk in recent years about the two cultures in Northern Ireland. But the only agency which has seriously and consistently attempted to explain one group or tradition to the other has been the schools service of the BBC. Those of us involved in education owe a great deal to James Hawthorne and his associates, whose integrity, tolerance and obvious attempts at objectivity raised them above suspicion or controversy.[19]

At least we tried.

NOTES

1. The BBC Handbook for 1961, reporting on the year 1960, noted that there were was a team of fifteen full-time Education Officers in various parts of the country 'whose job is to report on the broadcasts and to maintain close liaison between the classroom and the broadcasting studio . . .'By the time Northern Ireland got its first series, Scotland and Wales each had eight, of which six were in the Welsh language. (BBC Handbook 1963).
2. The incumbent 'Assistant Head of Programmes, Northern Ireland' was Rev Robert Crossett, an excellent broadcaster in his own right but inexperienced as a producer and uncomfortable as a manager. He died of a heart attack in October 1961 while still in post.
3. Shortly after my arrival, the Head of Educational Broadcasting's status was elevated to that of Controller.
4. In those days the term 'radio' had not yet replaced 'sound' in BBC professional jargon. Norman Lloyd Williams was Head of Schools Broadcasting (Sound) and Ivan Gilman rejoiced in 'Chief Assistant Schools Broadcasting (Sound)'. Lloyd Williams was my inspiration and Gilman a stalwart guide in my early career.
5. Schools Broadcasting Council for the united Kingdom (SBC) paper 9/61.
6. SBC Paper – Minutes of the NI Programme Subcommittee, 22 February 1961.
7. SBC Paper NI 14/62.
8. SBC paper NI 26/64.
9. SBC Paper NI 20/63
10. ibid.
11. As submitted in SBC paper NI 23/64 to the Northern Ireland Programme Subcommittee on 5 May 1964.

12. SBC NI Programme Subcommittee minutes 5 May 1964
13. BBC schools programmes originating from Northern Ireland were placed among the outstanding educational successes of 1965; 'a mathematics series of remarkable charm and humour' and 'a series for schools in Northern Ireland, Two Centuries of Irish History'. (BBC Handbook 1966).
14. WR Hutchison, Norman Harrison, Bill Meek, David Hammond, Gerard Hayes-McCoy and Martin Wallace. David Hammond researched and recorded most of the music.
15. From the BBC's Information Service at the time – the newspapers referred to were the *Belfast Telegraph*, the *Irish News* and the *Irish Times*.
16. SCB Paper NI 33/65. This was the last major committee paper to be written by the 'Education officer, North and Northern Ireland'. Leslie Davidson died in a London hospital in 1966.
17. Following appointments as the Government of Hong Kong's Controller of Television and Director of Broadcasting 1970-77. Appointed Controller BBC Northern Ireland 1 January 1978; retired 31 December 1987.
18. After years with only a programme subcommittee structure, the region acquired its own autonomous 'Schools Broadcasting Council for Northern Ireland' in 1978.
19. John Magee, Senior Research Fellow, Institute of Irish Studies, 1970. Lecture given at Queen's ; later published in *The Northern Teacher*.

CULTURE AND IDENTITY: THE BBC'S ROLE IN NORTHERN IRELAND

Pat Loughrey

I want, here, to address the cultural role of the BBC in Northern Ireland, and to relate that to the agenda of the wider Corporation. What follows are necessarily my subjective thoughts on what is a very complex topic. Many of the issues raised deserve a great deal more research and reflection.

The BBC's cultural remit in Northern Ireland is the same as that of the wider BBC. While I, like many other people, have been tempted to smile at the old BBC notion of 'giving the people what's good for them', there is still something honourable about the notion of bringing the creative best in this country into every home in the land. To bring Shakespeare and serious music to everyone, regardless of their class or income, is a worthy aspiration. I do not think that we should be as apologetic as we sometimes are about the Reithian mission. There is something valid about it still. I do not believe that there has been a real democratisation of cultural life. Serious music and quality theatre are no more accessible to the vast bulk of people now than they were in the 1920s. There is therefore still a need for the BBC to bring the best of cultural life to everyone for the minimal charge of the licence fee. The function of the BBC's national regions is to ensure that our understanding of this cultural life is not too narrow or too metropolitan. The activities which we nurture should not only be evaluated from the centre.

I'm constantly inspired by the Monaghan poet Patrick Kavanagh. In his poem *Epic*, he describes a row over half a rood of rock, 'a no-man's land', surrounded by pitchfork-armed claimants.

> That was the year of the Munich bother. Which
> Was more important? I inclined
> To lose my faith in Ballyrush and Gortin

Till Homer's ghost came whispering to my mind
He said: I made the Iliad from such
A local row. Gods make their own importance.

It is terribly important that the deities within the BBC, and espe-
cially the BBC in Northern Ireland, should never lose faith in
Ballyrush and Gortin. The history of this region of the BBC is one
of a faltering coming to terms with local identity in all its diversity.
The greatest contributions were made by a few individuals. The
BBC made space for some quite remarkable talents – Tyrone
Guthrie, Denis Johnston, Louis MacNeice, Bertie Rogers, Sam
Hanna Bell, Havelock Nelson, David Hammond. There is a long
list of dedicated people who were less than submissive to the establishment, and who passionately believed in the value of their own
place. They determined to nurture local culture, often in an
intemperate climate in this community. At best they were icono-
clastic, innovative and pioneering; at worst they were self-indul-
gent, sometimes elitist and often given to wishful thinking. Melvyn
Bragg described his time working with Louis MacNiece and Bertie
Rogers in Broadcasting House, London, in the late 1950s. They
spent a great deal of their time in the George public house, and
anyone who appeared in the office on more than two consecutive
days was considered a sissy. It was a fine Patrician world they inhab-
ited.

When the BBC was established in 1922, it had to find its place
alongside the new state of Northern Ireland. The British
Broadcasting Company, as it was then, was not, at first, particularly
keen to come to Northern Ireland. It tried to avoid the cultural
and political minefield that broadcasting here would mean. But a
forceful local lobby won the day and the first premises were
opened in Linenhall Street. Those in authority decided to take a
few precautionary measures. Prime among them was to ensure
that mainly English and Scottish staff were appointed. Most of
those early programmes turned out to be uninspiring and uncontroversial.

But let us not commit an historiographical error by using contemporary yardsticks to judge a very different era. As we look at
Northern Ireland in the 1920s, it is wrong to use modern standards to measure success or failure. The 1920s was a time of rapid
cultural appropriation: the nation state in the South was emerging
and claiming for itself every aspect of Gaelic identity and

Northern Ireland was coming to terms with two conflicting nationalisms. One nationalist ideology claimed exclusive rights to Gaelic games, Irish music and the Irish language while the other, the Unionists, sought to monopolise the fife and drum and the whole Irish military tradition.

Cultural appropriation made the role of public service broadcaster exceptionally demanding for the BBC in Northern Ireland. Broadcasters, intentionally or unintentionally, tend to nurture the national myth. Alan Yentob, Controller BBC 1, recently spoke, fairly convincingly, of the National Lottery as a new national event which only the BBC should bring to the public. In the same way, the Grand National, the Boat Race and Wimbledon have been taken from relative obscurity and turned into national events, part of what it means to be British. In Scotland, the BBC and Andy Stewart together have defined Hogmanay for us. But what does it mean to be Northern Irish? What are the defining events? What are the great occasions that the public service broadcaster can bring into every home to inspire patriotism and a sense of belonging?

Back in 1924, Tyrone Guthrie thought he had the answer – St. Patrick's Day. He brought ceilidh nights to the airwaves and, long before they were ever heard in Dublin, pioneering productions by the Abbey Theatre Company. But, gradually, as a result of Unionist indignation, those early efforts were marginalised. Rex Cathcart observes 'the divided communities were adopting their preferred cultural stance'.[1] St. Patrick's night was turned into yet another evening for bland dance music. As the 1920s wore on, the results of Gaelic games, originally broadcast on a Sunday, were discontinued. Interestingly, hardly a word of criticism was heard from Catholic Ulster. It did not seem to have very high expectations of the BBC.

Broadcasting pioneers in Belfast suffered from social as well as sectarian prejudice. The voice of urban Protestant Belfast was consistently excluded from the airwaves. The sensibilities of the Ulster bourgeoisie were carefully guarded. When a local accent was heard, critics would typically ask 'What must the world think of Ulster?' In a display of pure provincialism, they worried not so much about what they were hearing, but rather what the rest of Britain might think of us. That kind of insecurity and middle-class intolerance bred a rather narrow social perspective for the first couple of decades of the BBC in Belfast.

Yet creative work was going on inside the new Broadcasting

House. W F Marshall, Presbyterian minister of Sixmilecross in Tyrone, was writing a wonderful series of radio talks called *Ulster Speaks*, asserting the purity of the Ulster tongue. He urged Ulster Protestants to take pride in their own heritage; not to ape the ways of the Home Counties, and to use the BBC in Belfast as a focus for their growing self-esteem. Marshall was many years ahead of his time. After the war, Henry McMullen was appointed as Programme Director, and Sam Hanna Bell became Features Producer. More than any other individual, Sam Bell established the cultural values of BBC Northern Ireland. I believe he helped this community to begin to understand itself. With Bertie Rogers and Louis MacNiece in London, new moulds were made. To epitomise their vision, a version of *A Midsummer Night's Dream* was recorded in a pure Tyrone dialect. They believed that only Tyrone preserved anything approaching the authentic Shakespearean English – a linguistic fossil left here from Elizabethan times. Appropriately, the production was introduced by W F Marshall. To lapse into anecdote again, there's a story about the recording of *Lily Bolero*, written and produced by Denis Johnston. To add to the authenticity, they brought a Lambeg drummer into the studio. Such was the volume of the Lambeg drum, it had to be put in a separate studio in the basement. The drummer was given the classic instruction 'just you keep drumming while the red light's on'. They duly switched the light on during the live performance and the man began drumming. When the production team was on its way to the club, having congratulated each other on another successful night, they heard an unearthly drumming still going on. They went into the studio and found this unfortunate man with blood streaming down both wrists. They had forgotten to switch the red light off.

In 1947 Billy Boucher was appointed as Music Producer and an energetic Scot, Andrew Stewart, became Controller. Together they succeeded in creating the Northern Ireland Orchestra. The Orchestra was, and is to this day, of enormous significance in bringing the very best of music-making to Northern Ireland.

Stewart also offered support to the increasing enterprise of Sam Hanna Bell. Sam, complete with what was then the latest in technology, the mobile recording unit, set out to bring the authentic voice of Ulster to the airways. As he himself said, 'Up to this time the working class voice had never been heard in Broadcasting House, Belfast'.

Sam Bell went to Queens Island and to every glen in the Sperrins with his recording machine. By contemporary broadcasting standards, that material was rigidly scripted and stilted but in its time it was wonderfully innovative and enriching. Sean O'Boyle's collection of Ulster songs and Michael J Murphy' s work on Ulster folklore are now of great archival value. Andrew Stewart must also be thanked for *The McCooeys*, the soap opera which is remembered fondly all over Ulster. Joe Tomelty's scripts now seem standard kitchen drama, but in their time they brought everyday life to the airways. They celebrated the *craic*. After Tomelty's tragic accident, that series proved impossible to replace.

In the early 1960s, came the creation of a department out of which I myself came – Educational Broadcasting. In the wider BBC, educational broadcasting is often slightly peripheral. In Northern Ireland however, educational issues regarding culture and identity are crucial. When Jimmy Hawthorne was appointed as the first schools producer, his background as a mathematician was perhaps reassuring to insecure executives. Jimmy characteristically broke out of the stereotype and created the first series of Irish history programmes to be shared in every school in Northern Ireland. In *Two Centuries of Irish History* he provided pioneering work of enormous significance. Educational Broadcasting continues to make pioneering programmes, on the environment, literature, Irish history and mythology. It provided the first Irish language output from any broadcaster in Northern Ireland.

When television came along, it was at first overshadowed by the radio service. Local television offered only *Country Ceilidh*, the *Half Door Club*, and a lot of pretty undemanding entertainment. It took quite a while for television here to find it's feet. Among the emerging television stars was James Young, a graduate of *The McCooeys*. When the story of that period is written, I believe James Young will be seen as a major figure. I for one will never forget his weekly entreaty 'Will you stop fighting'. He was a very shrewd judge of this place and of all our hidden prejudices.

When the nightmare of the last twenty five years dawned, it found the media ill-prepared. If consciously or unconsciously we had laboured towards some kind of consensus, then we, and many other well-intentioned bodies, failed. One part of that failure was the sense of alienation felt by the Protestant working class, and to some extent that alienation continues today. Jackie Redpath, in his submission to the Opsahl commission, said that 'the Protestant working class culture is rubbished in the media, no-one defends it'.[2] There is a sense of disenfranchisement and a sense of alienation among working class Protestants that we must confront and explore. Arthur Aughey has said that what is distinctive of political Protestantism – its Orange marches, its flute bands, its large banners, its sectarian songs – is taken as the sum total of all cultural life in that community. That is like taking the Free Presbyterian church to be the sum total of Protestant religious life. A media shorthand of easy symbols can be damaging and dangerous.

We must also ensure that the media does not project a narrow definition of culture. Too many of us come from a humanities background. We tend to neglect material culture. The whole world of Ulster innovation, industry, business, and technology tends to be overlooked. In doing so we turn our backs on core defining characteristics of Ulster identity. The BBC has a duty to celebrate, promote, explore, and even to define cultural identity. We have done a great deal. Those pioneering efforts, judged by the yardsticks of their own time, were significant and influential. I believe that at this time of unprecedented change we have an obligation to maintain that pioneering spirit and to continue to guide the definition of self in this community.

BBC Northern Ireland today is founded on the same principles as in Lord Reith's time. We are committed to enrich the lives of our audiences. As life in this society changes, so must the services we offer. Our schedule today is totally different from the past. Ulster accents are to be heard throughout the day on local television and radio. Depending on your taste and needs, BBC Northern Ireland is trustworthy and challenging News and Current Affairs; Home Truths documentaries; George Jones in the afternoon; Ulster Orchestra concerts; Irish Language dramas; the Hole in the Wall Gang's comedy; Sean Coyle on BBC Foyle; and much more television drama than ever before. As the range and quality of what we do expands, so does our confidence in the significance of our own identity. BBC Northern Ireland provides the only direct platform for the local voice on the national networks.

I am convinced that this confidence will continue to grow, and that BBC Northern Ireland will go on making a significant contribution to local and national life through an unrivalled range and quality of programmes.

NOTES

1. Rex Cathcart, *The Most Contrary Region: The BBC in Northern Ireland 1924-84* (Belfast: Blackstaff Press, 1984).
2. Andy Pollak (ed.), *A Citizens' Inquiry: The Opsahl Report on Northern Ireland* (Dublin: The Lilliput Press, 1993), p.44.

DRAMA OUT OF A CRISIS: BBC TELEVISION DRAMA AND THE NORTHERN IRELAND TROUBLES.

Martin McLoone

In retrospect, 1993 now looks like an important transitional year in the recent history of Northern Ireland. It was a year in which the tragic and the hopeful existed side by side, plunging many people from high optimism to the depths of despair, and back again, almost by the day. It was the year of such tragedies as the Warrington bombing, the Shankill Road bombing and the Greysteel massacre. But it was also the year of the Hume/Adams talks, the year in which the government finally admitted that it had 'opened channels of communication with Sinn Féin' and the year which ended with the Downing Street Declaration, signed by both the Irish and British governments. It was the year, in other words, which paved the way for the 1994 ceasefires and yet which witnessed some of the worst acts of brutal violence which the ceasefires were designed to bring to an end.

It was also something of a transitional year for television representations of paramilitary violence. Two aspects of this, in particular, are worth noting. First, in the NIO anti-terrorist advertisements, shown only in Northern Ireland itself, there was a clear shift in perspective in the way in which, what are effectively government propaganda films, chose to portray the perpetrators of the violence. In a series of three short films promoting the confidential telephone number, the violence was shown with new levels of graphic intensity, mimicking the special effects style of mainstream cinematic thrillers. However, the male perpetrators of this violence were shown for the first time as ordinary family men, with wives and children to love and look after. The faceless hooded figures of previous campaigns, seemingly driven by psychological problems or sheer criminal malevolence, were gone. In the 1993 campaign, the gunmen are handsome, trendy and in all

respects ordinary, 'normal' young men. There is a tacit acceptance, at the very least, that these men are driven, not by psychopathology, but by political principles, even if the victims of
their political commitment are ultimately the women and the children who validate them as human beings in the first place.[1]

These advertisements ran through the Summer of 1993, and in
September of that year there was another significant shift in perspective, this time in regard to television drama. Ronan Bennett's
political thriller *Love Lies Bleeding* (directed by Michael
Winterbottom) reached the small screen amid an unprecedented
splurge of advance publicity and pre-emptive speculation. Shown
on BBC 2 on Wednesday 22 September, it was contextualised the
previous evening by a *Late Show* special, *Telling the Troubles,* which
looked at over twenty years of fictional representations of the situation in Northern Ireland; on the Monday evening, a short BBC
NI piece, *Re-making the Maze,* looked at various aspects of the making of the film (concentrating on the set specially built in a disused
factory to shoot the scenes set in the H-blocks of the Maze prison)
and, over the previous weekend, there was a plethora of newspaper features anticipating the likely outcry over the film's unusually
sympathetic portrait of the IRA.[2]

There can be no doubt that Bennett's film was a major departure for television drama, concentrating as it did on the IRA and
its attempt to purge from its ranks those hard-liners opposed to
the organisation's strategy of ending the conflict and starting talks
with the British government. The film slowly built empathy with
the IRA leaders and especially with Conn, the volunteer at the centre of the drama. The political context in which republicanism
operates, and the level of popular support which it enjoys within
its own communities, is clearly shown. So too is the organisation's
capacity for brutal violence in pursuit of its political aims and the
film's denouement is a graphically portrayed and carefully chore-
ographed massacre of the hard-line element. Yet interestingly
enough, the film generated little controversy – indeed, if anything, there was an overly generous and enthusiastic response to a
film that, despite the all-round competence of its production and
its unusually interesting theme, nonetheless, strained credulity in
purely dramatic terms. Even more interesting is the fact that in the
end, Bennett's film hardly progressed the view of political violence
beyond that which had been insinuating itself into the popular
consciousness all that Summer in the NIO advertisements. It

seemed that, at last, there was real or tacit acceptance that, despite its savagery and pitiless nature, violence in Northern Ireland was ultimately politically motivated and the politics of the situation would eventually have to be confronted.

The reception afforded to *Love Lies Bleeding* is in sharp contrast to the furore that followed the screening in January 1989 of Alan Clarke's *Elephant* (directed by Danny Boyle), which, according to newspaper reports at the time, drew an unprecedented number of complaints to the BBC from outraged viewers throughout Britain as well as in Northern Ireland.[3] Press reviews of the film, whether the national broadsheets or tabloids or the local unionist press, vied to come up with the most vitriolic condemnations. Clarke's film is a much more intensely ambiguous piece than Bennett's and is, in some regards, the complete antithesis of what Bennett set out to do.[4] It is a short forty-minute piece which re-enacts eighteen brutal murders, one after the other, without narrative or character motivation. Each murder follows a similar pattern. The camera picks up and follows a character in an everyday setting (a swimming pool, a park, a taxi-rank, a petrol station or an ordinary home) and follows him until he either cold-bloodedly kills or is himself the victim of an unexplained, seemingly motiveless killing. After each shooting, the camera dwells on the body of the victim for an excruciatingly long time, before the next cycle of killing is introduced.

At the time, the BBC publicity explained the title as a reference to the fact that it is as difficult to ignore the Northern Ireland troubles as it is to ignore the presence of an elephant in your own sitting-room. Yet the film surely argues the opposite – that if the elephant is there long enough and an explanation of its presence withheld for long enough, then, unlikely as it might seem, its presence no longer excites much interest. In other words, the catalogue of unexplained and seemingly motiveless violence, removed from any explanatory framework, becomes an unpleasant and totally misunderstood phenomenon that people accept as part of their mental landscape. It holds no prospect of being resolved because it no longer seems extraordinary enough to demand sufficient attention. In this regard, the film can be seen as an attack on the way in which the media, especially television news, has covered the violence, rendering it as a nightly catalogue of seemingly aimless and unmotivated atrocities. The ambiguity of the film rests in the fact that it then reproduces the very situation

which it sets out to criticise – a catalogue of random, de-contextu-
alised killings.

The film proved to be such a demanding piece, not only
because of the disturbing nature of the violence it depicted, but
also because it withholds from the audience the kind of narrative
coherence and character identification which is central to the
operation of conventional drama. It is an avant-garde piece, in
other words, in the sense that it choses to jettison normal artistic
rules and to challenge the television audience aesthetically as well
as politically. Thus, despite the undoubted breakthrough which
Love Lies Bleeding represented, and which was much trumpeted by
the press at the time, in retrospect, *Elephant* now seems a much
braver and more challenging break with the conventional dramatic modes of representing Northern Ireland.

Both films, then, are concerned to raise questions about the
nature of media representations and through their status as television drama, to do so, in particular, in relation to television
fiction. Most debates about media representations of Northern
Ireland have concentrated on news and current affairs coverage
and there is now a considerable body of literature which has dealt
with these issues.[5] The question of drama, however, is less well covered, and this is somewhat surprising, given the amount of television drama over the years which has addressed the Northern
Ireland situation in one form or another. I can identify over one
hundred titles of single dramas and series and I don't suppose that
this list is complete (see appendix 1). If one then adds the number of episodes of otherwise unrelated series which have tackled
the subject over the years (obvious ones like *The Professionals* and
less obvious examples like the BBC's series about an all-women
taxi-cab company, *Rides,* which set one episode in Derry and
Donegal) then the number of examples is very substantial indeed.

What is interesting about this range of drama is the fact that
over eighty per cent of it was made by the BBC and in this regard,
the Corporation can feel justified in claiming that it has performed its public service responsibilities well in response to such
an important and controversial issue. It might also be justified in
claiming that the quality and seriousness of its drama stands well
in comparison to the more exploitative approach of much of commercial television's output. I think it is important to register here
this hugely important contribution made by BBC drama over the
years – without it, dramatised accounts of Northern Ireland would

look decidedly threadbare. Perhaps as well, the dominance of news and current affairs in the controversies over media coverage of Northern Ireland has, to a large extent, disguised the sheer volume of dramatic representations. Thus, despite its achievements, television drama about Northern Ireland seems to have appeared only fleetingly in the schedules when compared to the almost nightly news and current affairs reporting. It is also valid, though, to argue that if there are dominant themes and characteristic modes of representation evident across this range of dramatic material, then the BBC, for better or ill, is also largely responsible.

Given the amount of drama produced, I do not intend here to give a definitive or a comprehensive appraisal. Although I have seen most of the drama produced, I have by no means seen it all. What I intend to do here is to offer ways of approaching, classifying and perhaps understanding the nature of the drama produced and of gauging its political significance. I want to concentrate on BBC drama but given the preponderance of the BBC in the field, I do not think that this will misrepresent unduly the dominant themes and style of the overall output.

Television Drama and Northern Ireland:
Some Recurring Themes

Although there has always a tradition of locally-produced radio drama at the BBC, there was no television drama from Belfast until the mid-1970s. This does not, of course, mean that there was no television drama about Northern Ireland at all. During the 1960s, in what is often referred to as 'the golden age' of television drama, there was a handful of plays produced centrally in both the BBC and the ITV network which addressed the political issues of Northern Ireland. The most celebrated of these was Granada's 1961 production of Sam Thompson's controversial anti-sectarian stage play, *Over the Bridge*, but there was a number of other early attempts at dramatising Northern Ireland, including another play by Sam Thompson, *Cemented With Love* (BBC, 1965), two plays by John D. Stewart, *Danger, Men Working* (Armchair Theatre, ABC, 1961) and *Boatman Do Not Tarry* (Playhouse, Ulster Television, 1968) and Alun Owen's *Progress to the Park* (Theatre 625, BBC, 1965). *Over the Bridge* had already caused considerable controversy when it was first produced for the stage in Belfast and Thompson's call for working-class solidarity across the sectarian divide probably reflected very well the optimism of the time, when the

Protestant working-class, at least, showed itself willing to vote for the Northern Ireland Labour Party (NILP) and move beyond the traditional sectarian politics of Ulster Unionism. By the end of the decade, with Paisleyism in the ascendancy and the NILP practically defunct, the rather downbeat portrayal of sectarian politics in Alun Owen's piece was to prove the more prescient.

Progress to the Park now looks more typical as well of both the status of Northern Ireland within British culture and politics of the time and as a taster of some of the dominant themes that were to emerge in the drama of the succeeding decades. Although the sectarian tensions of Northern Ireland are at the centre of the play's concerns, Owen pursues these as they manifest themselves in his native Liverpool, rather than in Northern Ireland itself, reflecting the totally marginal place occupied by Northern Ireland in the culture and politics of Britain in the 1960s. Owen follows a weekend in the lives of a group of young Liverpool people whose upbringing has been dominated by the sectarian bitterness of their parents. Two themes in particular emerge here which recur again and again in television drama about the North. First, there is a generational struggle, as the young are presented with the dilemma of either accepting or rejecting the political culture of their parents. For Owen, this is a key question and in some ways Liverpool itself represents the problem. The city is both a source of inspiration and strength but it is also backward, stifling and constricting. His characters leave in reality (the men are sailors, returning to Liverpool for a period of shore leave) or they leave in their fantasies (about London, Montreal or Africa). They carry with them, however, the attitudes that the city (and their parents) instilled in them since childhood and it is these attitudes that both nourish and debilitate them.

The second theme is the hardy perennial of Northern Ireland drama, the Romeo and Juliet syndrome. Mag Keegan and Billy Loughlin are in love, but she is Catholic and he is Protestant. Their blossoming romance was broken up five years earlier by their bitterly sectarian families (and there is a clear implication that this is what drove Billy to sea in the first place). The play traces their attempt to rekindle this love as adults against the strongly expressed wishes of their respective families. There is, in the characterisation of Billy and Mag, also an implication that they carry in their own hearts, too much of the sectarian bitterness of their parents for their love to succeed (though this is seen to be a much

greater problem for the Protestant Billy than the Catholic Mag).
Like all 'Romeo and Juliet' scenarios, the emphasis is on the
effects of a family feud on the young (and on the very notion of
'love' itself). There is, however, no exploration of why the respective households are feuding in the first place. As a comment on
the politics of Northern Ireland, the thwarted love scenario can
only work by jettisoning the politics in the first place.

Owen is not, however, an apolitical dramatist and *Progress to the
Park* has a rational, secular view-point. The dramatic centre of the
play is Billy's friend, Teifion, a Welsh-Liverpudlian carrying auto-
biographical echoes of Owen himself (and played by Peter
McEnery, who had played a similar alter-ego character in Owen's
play for *Armchair Theatre* in 1960, *Lena, O My Lena*). At various
points in the play, Teifion performs the role of Greek chorus or
Shakespearean fool, commenting on the other characters and on
the unfolding drama, sometimes in sly direct address to camera.
The message of the play is thus mediated through Teifion's commentary and it is hardly surprising when he articulates a basic
humanist rejection of the 'ancient quarrels' of the Irish. The
Liverpool Irish, he notes, 'are the best Catholics, the best
Protestants and the worst Christians in the world'. (Thus the feuding fathers arrive at the Sunday newspaper-seller together, barking
their order in unison – *'News of the World!'* Keegan then loudly adds
for the benefit of his orange neighbour, 'And *The Catholic
Herald!'*). This humanist message is another recurring element in
the television drama of later years and again, it achieves its force
by not only rejecting the sectarian politics of Northern Ireland but
by failing to deal with politics altogether. Finally, it might also be
noted that Owen raises a basic dichotomy between tradition and
modernity, represented by Teifion as a contrast between Liverpool
and London. Like much of the intellectual musings in the play,
this contrast is complex and ambiguous. If Liverpool tradition is
seen as the suffocating heritage of a long-gone past, then the
promise of modernity in Teifion's reminiscences of London are
seen to be the highly exaggerated imaginings of male bragging.
Nonetheless, despite the many accomplishments of Liverpool's
traditional culture and despite the obvious dangers of moving out
into an unknown world, the play finally vindicates the secular
humanist politics of modernity over the dead hand of the past.
This message too was to reappear in many of the television plays
and films which were to follow.

Owen's play is very much of its time – naturalist studio drama, shot very economically on videotape and depending on the the-atrical elements of acting and writing at the expense of visual sophistication or elaborate mise-en-scène. It is also a very British play, in that it explores the clash of differing cultures and genera-tions, with a strong emphasis on challenging paternalistic author-ity. In its treatment of Irish themes, it bears a strong resemblance to John McGrath's *Incident at the Bofor's Gun* (filmed by Jack Gold as *The Bofor's Gun* in 1968) and especially *The Reckoning* (1969, again by McGrath and Gold) in both of which the main Irish char-acter was played by Nicol Williamson. The Irish element here is used to construct 'the other' to the straight-laced sense of Britishness which is being probed and the centre of dramatic ten-sion is the contradictions of Britishness rather than any serious dramatic exploration of Irishness. It is hardly surprising, then, that the Irishness which does emerge tends to be rather hackneyed.

As far as mainstream British culture was concerned in the 1960s, Northern Ireland itself was an obscure and unknown periphery, little acknowledged and rarely featuring as prime time television material. After October 1968, when the news programmes of the world carried RTE's pictures of the bloody attack by the RUC on the Civil Rights marchers in Duke Street in Derry, Northern Ireland moved into the centre of British politics and continued to dominate the news and current affairs agenda for more than two decades. It took much longer for television drama to come to terms with the crisis, however. Even as late as 1980, a full twelve years after the initial upsurge of violence, radical television drama-tist Trevor Griffith was lamenting the paucity of drama which attempted to address the situation in Northern Ireland. At a con-ference held at Goldsmiths College that year, 'The Television Play and Contemporary Society', the documentation included a reprint of Richard Hoggart's contribution to a recent *South Bank Show* discussion on television drama and Northern Ireland in which he had claimed that there had only been nineteen plays in twelve years on a Northern Ireland theme. Griffith used this piece by Hoggart to launch an attack on the poor response of television drama to what he considered to be the outstanding political ques-tion in contemporary British politics. In its report of this confer-ence, *Television Today* rather laments the way in which Griffith 'hijacked' the conference to raise questions about Northern Ireland, but this does, nonetheless, point to the fact that there was still a reluctance on behalf of the various television companies to fully engage with Northern Ireland in dramatic terms.[6]

What Hoggart and Griffith could not detect at the time was that the impetus to dramatise aspects of the Northern Ireland crisis had already started to gather momentum. Over the next fifteen years, the subject appeared increasingly more regularly as a topic for television drama across a diverse range of genres. There can be no doubt that the increasing commitment of the BBC, especially in Northern Ireland, was a major factor in this process. Before looking more closely at the post-1960s drama, it is important to consider some of the production contexts within television itself which brought this about, as well as looking at the changing political context of Northern Ireland, against which this drama was produced.

The Changing Contexts

If we take October 1968 as the turning point, when the local rumblings burst into national and international consciousness, then I think we need to locate television drama about Northern Ireland within a number of contexts that have changed substantially over the intervening twenty-seven years. We might schematise these in this way:

1. The pace of the political events themselves and the way in which these impinged on broadcasting generally.
2. The changing nature of government policy over the years and the way in which this impinged on broadcasting culture generally.
3. The debate about public service broadcasting over this period and especially the increasing demand from the BBC regions for greater autonomy to originate and produce television drama for the network but which, nonetheless, is conceived initially to address local concerns.
4. The changing nature of television drama production itself, from the ascendancy of the studio-based single play of the 1960s, to the television film of the 1990s, conceived with cinema-release potential in mind.
5. The changing contexts of academic analysis of the conflict, especially the tendency in recent years to look beyond a merely British/Irish context and to locate Northern Ireland within an international perspective on ethnic and national conflict.

These contexts themselves interact with the types of drama which have emerged and, again a little schematically, we might note three broad categories into which this drama has fallen: thrillers, drama/documentary and authored drama (or the single play – in some senses, the distance travelled in the evolution of the single drama can be gauged by a tendency that has seen the author of the drama replaced by the director of the film as the recognised controlling vision of the piece – a move from the theatricality of the single play to the cinematic status of the television film). Like all such broad categorisations, this scheme can appear too prescriptive – many of these categories overlap, so that, for example, in the case of *Love Lies Bleeding*, the format is an investigative thriller and there can be little doubt that the authorial voice was located with the writer, Ronan Bennett, rather than with the director, Michael Winterbottom. In the case of the BBC's two attempts at comedy (*Foreign Bodies*, 1987-89 and *So You Think You Have Troubles*, 1991) a genre – the sit com – which is rarely associated with such a complex and disturbing topic, was attempted. But as a broad descriptive tool, it has its use as a set of general contexts in which the drama output of the BBC, and its recurring themes outlined earlier, might better be assessed.

BBC Television Drama:
An Overview

With *the thriller*, the situation in Northern Ireland is used merely as a backdrop to a plot which operates in a purely conventional manner. This type of drama has been mostly the preserve of commercial television and was inaugurated by Yorkshire Television's *Harry's Game*, (1982), scripted by ex-journalist, Gerald Seymour and directed by Lawrence Gordon Clark. The Northern Ireland setting is used mainly because it provides some of the essential elements to thriller plot lines – double agents, double dealing, dirty tricks and the potential for a conflict of interest, especially where love across the divide can be worked in. *Harry's Game* achieved this admirably – other examples were both poor thrillers and risible in their treatment of the Northern Ireland setting (Channel 4's *The Price*, 1985 or Yorkshire's more recent *Circle of Deceit*, 1993). The fact that the setting is merely a plot device does not, however, exonerate even the best of these from accusations of exploitation or of peddling the same hoary old clichés about Northern Ireland. Indeed, in their treatment of paramilitaries, almost always republican, these thrillers manage to exacerbate the problem by denying the political dimension to the conflict, neatly dove-tailing the 'official' line that these men are psychopaths or criminals. In the one thriller which is largely concerned with loyalist paramilitaries, Central's co-production with New Zealand television, *The Grasscutter* (1989), loyalism is linked to sexual deviancy and incest, as well as to psychopathology (although in truth, the film, if it was about anything, was about the beauty of its New Zealand locations, lovingly filmed in aerial photography and endless tracking shots).

BBC drama has been less inclined to exploit the situation for the purposes of 'mere entertainment', though in *Love Lies Bleeding*, the political potential of the thriller format, and especially of its investigative plot line, is utilised effectively to deliver both an efficient thriller and an interesting exploration of the politics of the situation. Less successful was *Final Run* (BBC, 1988) which used the same plot device (the relocation under an assumed identity of a supergrass witness) as the much more glossy *The Grasscutter* and Television South's co-production with Australian broadcasters, *Act of Betrayal* (1988). But unlike Bennett's film, *Final Run* downplays both the thriller elements and the politics to concentrate on the pressures on the family of a situation in which every day must be lived as a lie and in fear of being discovered. Closer in spirit to Bennett's film was the BBC's four-part adaptation of MS Power's trilogy about the IRA, *Children of the North* (1991). The screening of this serial was postponed from its original date because the BBC deemed it inappropriate during the Gulf War to screen a programme that suggested a certain kinship between the machinations of the IRA and their counterparts in military intelligence. When it was finally screened later in the year, it somehow failed to make the kind of impact that such a major production is expected to and which perhaps the interesting marriage of its literary roots, thriller form and political speculation deserved. The scenario, in fact, is similar to *Love Lies Bleeding* – the problems within the IRA between the 'hawks and doves' – though to be honest, the image that emerged is of a shadowy world of cross and double-cross on all sides, where the only politics are the politics of bluff, betrayal and misinformation. In the end, the generic requirements of the thriller form can conspire against its use as a dramatic mechanism for dealing with politics, even when, as was the case with Ken Loach's film *Hidden Agenda*

(1989), the politics are more overt than is normally the case with the thriller.[7]

Drama/documentary (or documentary/drama, depending on the balance which is attempted between 'real' events and the fiction-alised mode) is more closely aligned to events in the real world, and to their mediation through news and current affairs. It is hardly surprising, therefore, that this type of production, whether set in a Northern Irish context or not, has been at the centre of controversy almost continuously over the years. It might also be noted in this context that the interplay between the factual and the fictional mode became increasingly more complex during this long period. If dramatists moved to incorporate elements of news and current affairs reporting into their fictional universe (a tendency at least as old as Orson Welles' production of *The War of the Worlds* for American radio in 1939), then it became increasingly more common for news, current affairs and documentary producers to incorporate fictional reconstruction within their factual universe.

One of the earliest controversies over dramatic portrayals of Northern Ireland involved precisely such a dramatic reconstruction, *Willie – The Legion Hall Bombing* (BBC, *Play For Today*, 1978). The script by Caryl Churchill was edited from the actual transcripts of the trial in a Belfast 'Diplock' court of Willie Gallagher, sentenced to twelve years for the bombing of the Strabane Legion Hall. A strong cast that included David Kelly and Niall Toibin, acted out the actual words of the transcript, interpreting in their own manner the characterisation which these suggested. The controversy, though, was not about matters of interpretation or re-interpretation but rather that the BBC changed the wording of a prologue, written specially by Churchill and director, Roland Joffé, and dropped altogether a similarly scripted epilogue.[8] The BBC's argument at the time was that the changes to the prologue were required in terms of accuracy and that the epilogue was tantamount to the BBC 'editorialising' on behalf of one interpretation (or 'verdict') and it was surely for viewers to make up their own minds on the basis of the evidence presented in the trial transcripts. For the production team, it was a clear case of political censorship and further evidence of BBC timidity in the face of establishment hostility. The fact that the original screening date for the production in February of 1978 had been cancelled because of the La Mon bombing in Belfast earlier that month only fuelled the controversy. Historically, it proved that drama could enjoy no privileged position where it was above the possibility of legal or other kinds of pressure and certainly not when it sailed so close to the concerns of news and current affairs.

Most of the drama/documentary controversies about Northern Ireland involved productions from the commercial channels, rather than the BBC – for example Channel 4's similar dramatising of a court transcript of the (failed) Birmingham Six appeal of 1988; Granada's *Who Bombed Birmingham?* (1990) and Yorkshire Television's *Shoot to Kill* (1990). It might be noted, too, that the BBC's dramatisation of the Maguire Seven case, *A Safe House* (1990) caused barely a ripple, the case having been blown wide open by that time. However, a couple of years earlier, the Corporation had passed on Tom McGurk's moving version of the same story, produced later by RTE as *Dear Sarah* (1990). Clearly, the closeness of the drama/doc to news and current affairs made it a troublesome genre for all television companies and given the centrality of this hybrid form to television drama generally over many years, it is perhaps surprising (or not) that so few have been made about Northern Ireland.

The *authored drama* (in the earlier period, synonymous with the single play) is by far and away the most common form of television drama and although once a feature of all British television drama, from the mid-1970s on, it became more associated with BBC drama only, as the commercial companies became conscious of its escalating costs and its declining hold on audience interest. The fact that the commercial companies were increasingly reluctant to invest in the single play as the 1970s turned into the 1980s threw the spotlight onto the BBC and gave rise to a recurring debate about the viability of the form itself (and the Goldsmiths College conference referred to earlier was only one manifestation of this debate). In 1983, the BBC put the matter into financial perspective. According to its own figures, although drama accounted for only six per cent of total BBC output, it consumed twenty-four per cent of annual costs (at about £170,000 per hour to produce).[9] By this time already, audience figures had begun to suggest that the popularity of the single play was on the decrease, causing David Cunliffe, then Controller of Drama at Yorkshire Television, to question the continuing viability of the form. 'If the viewer doesn't show much enthusiasm for the single play, how many of them can the programme companies afford?'[10]

In many ways the BBC sought to copper-fasten its public service credentials by its continuing support for the single drama but there were two other factors at play in the debate which it could hardly ignore. First, with the advent of Channel 4 in 1982 and the start of its *Film on Four* strand, it was obvious that the single play was already giving way to the television film and this raised a whole series of economic and aesthetic questions about the future direction of television drama.[11] The continuing practice of referring to the one-off drama as a 'play' had tended to obscure the fact, anyway, that most one-off television drama at the BBC was already being shot on film, and increasingly shot on location rather than in the studio. The transformation in drama aesthetics at the BBC was confirmed by 1987 when the then Head of Drama, Peter Goodchild, introduced the new *Screenplay* strand by declaring that the aim of the new strand was 'to get away as far as possible from the rather "static" feel of TV plays'[12] The other factor was the increasing pressure from the national regions of the BBC – Scotland, Wales and Northern Ireland – for the right to make drama specific to its national audiences, a pressure that had been building since the 1970s and became a top priority at the BBC in Belfast after 1978 when James Hawthorne took over as Controller. If the production of single drama was seen as the *sine qua non* of public service broadcasting, how much more so was the proper representation of regional differences and concerns? Of course, before BBC NI could get in on the act, there was a problem of getting anything about Northern Ireland onto the screen in the first place and the output of drama from any source was slow to begin with. However, under the prompting from Belfast, the pace of BBC drama certainly quickened with increasingly more being originated in Northern Ireland itself. The record of achievement is certainly impressive and the BBC nourished the careers of such distinguished dramatists as Stewart Parker, Graham Reid, Ann Devlin and Ron Hutchinson and produced many adaptations from writers like Jennifer Johnston, William Trevor, MS Power and Maurice Leitch. The success of many of these works is not in dispute here but I want to look at them through a focus on the question of politics, and especially on the issue of paramilitary violence, since it was this, it seems to me, that remained the great uninvestigated issue as far as news and current affairs was concerned. In the final analysis, the problem in Northern Ireland has always been, and continues to be, a *political* problem and it was this, rather than some inherent psychopathology, that caused the violence. How, then, did television drama deal with the politics of the situation?

As the political crisis in Northern Ireland deepened, and especially after the troops went on to the streets in 1969 (and began to suffer casualties almost immediately), the impact on broadcasting became increasingly more problematic and controversial.[13] This affected news and current affairs coverage in particular, and gave rise to a system of indirect, and then direct censorship, which culminated in the broadcasting ban on Sinn Féin and other organisations. As the situation became more fraught for the journalist, it might have seemed logical that the dramatist, especially the television dramatist who carried such prestige within the culture of British television, might be able to probe into areas where the journalist was constrained. To a large extent, this did not happen, especially where the question of paramilitary violence was concerned. Writing about the prestige enjoyed by the authored drama within British television, John Caughie has observed that the single play of the 1960s and 1970s was 'to function for television as some kind of cutting edge, working to extend television's social or sexual discourse'.[14] This is undoubtedly true, but it rarely functioned to extend a purely political discourse, and over the years, there are very few examples of television drama that worked in this fashion. One might say that it was at its most adventurous working in the ideological arena rather than in the political. Confronted with the complex politics of Northern Ireland, and especially with the question of political violence, then it had no ready genre or tradition to tap into. The politics of Northern Ireland were quite literally beyond the Pale.

This is a point well illustrated by the contrasting views of radical journalist, Eamonn McCann and one of the most prolific writers of drama for television, Graham Reid, in a feature in *Broadcast*.[15] For McCann, the problem was that most television drama was written from the metropolitan viewpoint that 'it's a terrible pity what's happening over there and if only the ordinary, decent people on both sides could get together.' He goes on to argue that 'since television drama must by its nature personalise issues, the standard theme, upon which variations are played, is of personal relationships being ripped apart by the sectarian divide. . .' He offers his own scenario of the kind of drama which the Northern Ireland crisis can suggest, built around the conflicting pressures and emotions which the mother of a dying hunger-striker must have had to endure.[16]

Reid, on the other hand, argues that what is dramatically significant about Northern Ireland is the fact that the people are no different from people anywhere else in the UK. To that extent, then, as a dramatist, 'Whatever subject I tackle, I will do so through human beings and through human relationships'. The writer, he feels, must avoid taking sides for fear of reinforcing already held prejudices. 'It is worth remembering . . . that a soapbox is not a very edifying visual image.' He clearly wants to carve out an imaginative space for the writer which is not circumscribed by the news and current affairs agenda nor hidebound by the need to offer a solution to the problem. 'In Northern Ireland there is no solution as such. There is a need for toleration.' [17]

Interestingly enough, both writers agree that part of the solution is to have more local drama produced out of Northern Ireland and both disagree fundamentally over the merits of Mike Leigh's *Four Days in July* (BBC, 1986). For Reid, despite Leigh's otherwise impressive career, as an outsider to Northern Ireland, he totally missed the point and ended up offering a perspective on the North which would only reinforce entrenched prejudices on all sides. For McCann, the value of Leigh's piece was that it avoided the perennial liberal desire to find a common ground between the opposing forces, allowing each side to speak in a way that the normal consensus-seeking agenda of most other television drama on the subject disguises. In a sense, I think both writers are correct. At the end of the play, the two women, Catholic Colette and Protestant Lorraine, have given birth and are in adjacent beds in the maternity ward. This has been the only point of contact between the two women and the scene is set up to have them discover their essential humanity in the shared experience of motherhood. But when they ask each other what names they will give their children, a cultural barrier comes down. The newborn babies may start with a clean sheet, but they will be educated and culturised differently.

This is, of course, a break with the liberal 'we are all only human beings after all' philosophy which has dominated the authored drama about Northern Ireland and the scene would have played very differently in a Graham Reid play. But Reid is correct to argue that the play is unbalanced, and I think this lies in an imbalance of audience identification throughout the play. The plot parallels

the lives of Colette's and Lorraine's families, especially their hus-
bands, Eugene and Billy, over the four days leading up to the
Twelfth and the birth of their respective children. In these bril-
liantly realised scenes, the Catholics have the best lines, the best
stories and the most heart-warming experiences, despite living
with the worst aspects of the violence. As Paul Clements has
argued, 'The film is a poetic meditation upon nationality and culture. . . . (Leigh's) sympathy is clearly with the Catholic side . . .
The manner of Eugene's and Colette's living embodies a greater
richness of warmth and humanity than is the case with Billy and
Colette. . . . contrasted are Billy's pessimism and sense of betrayal
. . . with the imaginative, life-affirming optimism and simple
hope of the Catholic couple.' Incredibly enough, Clements then
asserts that Leigh's view of the Catholic couple is neither senti-
mental or sentimentalised.[18] To my mind it is clearly both, though
presumably from a perspective like McCann's, it was not before
time that the working-class nationalist community in Northern
Ireland got a good press.

However, it is no good portraying sympathetically the community which gives active, and at the very least passive, support to the
IRA at the expense of demonising the community which equally
gives support to loyalist paramilitaries or at the very least to the
RUC and the Army. Both share a common humanity. The uncomfortable political reality is that this humanity is not enough to stop
them from distrusting and even violently abhorring the other side.
If the play is correct in seeing that the issue is not amenable to liberal wish-fulfilment, its own blinkered analysis glosses over the
harsh reality that throws this liberalism into crisis in the first place.

Four Days in July at least was prepared to go beyond the rhetoric
of a common humanity and embrace, at least on one side, the reality of the political culture of Northern Ireland. The general tendency, as McCann has argued and which Reid's comments
confirm, is to ignore the politics altogether. In many ways, this
became a sub-genre in itself, strongly laced with a variety of
Romeo and Juliet plotlines, which was guaranteed to evince critical praise in direct proportion to its distance from the uncomfortable reality. Thus Hazel Holt, reviewing Jennifer Johnston's
Shadows on our Skin (BBC, *Play for Today*, 1980), observed that it
'was not really about Northern Ireland: the troubles just happened to be there, souring everything as they do in real life.'[19]
John Wyver, reviewing Stewart Parker's *Iris in the Traffic, Ruby in the*

Rain (BBC, *Play for Today*, 1981), notes 'Warm and engagingly casual, Stewart Parker's film is a splendidly understated study of two ordinary lives in Belfast. The British Army continually intrudes in the background but Parker's concern is with his characters.' [20] Jennifer Lovelace, writing about Ron Hutchinson's *The Last Window Cleaner* (BBC, *Play for Today*, 1979) was somewhat bemused. 'Although political problems loomed constantly in the background, they were merely the starting point for Mr. Hutchinson's exploration of his characters' eccentricities, as they pursued their several ways, linked by their occupancy of a run-down boarding house set on an island in the midst of a sea of trouble.' [21] Finally, Jill Weekes, reviewing one of the BBC's earliest productions set in contemporary Northern Ireland, Martin Dillon's *The Squad* (BBC, *Centre Play Showcase*, 1976), touches on a key point.

> The problem of linking the atrocities in Belfast to ordinary human beings is probably insurmountable since it remains impossible to believe that ordinary sane people could generate such chaos. Better drama is written from the standpoint of, say, O' Casey where the chaos is a terrible but given fact and ordinary human beings are viewed against this background.[22]

The mention of O'Casey is apt, because many of the better-received and better-written dramas over the years, especially the plays of Graham Reid, and certainly Stewart Parker's intermittently brilliant *Pentecost* (BBC, Theatre Night, 1990), end up merely echoing O'Casey's humanist anguish about the absurdity of the violence. The difference was that when O'Casey was writing, the violence was finished and he was concerned with the heritage of those years and how this might impinge on the present. The continuing violence in Northern Ireland surely needed something more than this. It called out to be understood and addressed in its political context. It took too long for the realisation to set in that such chaos was, indeed, generated by ordinary people and that therefore there must be an extraordinary set of factors that pushed them to these extremes.

It is hardly surprising that a political crisis that has lasted for more than quarter of a century (and which still seems a long way from any kind of solution) should have generated a huge amount of academic analysis.[23] In recent years, certainly since the late 1980s, this academic literature has tended to stress the characteristics which Northern Ireland shares with other areas of conflict throughout the world. The emphasis has shifted – from seeing the problem as unique (to the historical relationship between Britain and Ireland) to seeing the situation as a locally inflected example of a more universal condition (concerning disputed notions of identity and involving ethnic conflict). This is a more significant universalising tendency than that of 'a common humanity' which has underpinned so much television drama about Northern Ireland over the years. It is a more political approach, designed to get closer to those (often unpleasant) political realities which lie at the heart of the Northern Ireland problem. The best drama, to my mind, is that which has come closest to probing, not the tragic circumstances for the 'Romeos and Juliets' of the world, but rather why the Capulets and the Montagues are 'at variance' in the first place.

The evidence from elsewhere in recent years, from Bosnia to Rwanda, confirms that under extraordinary political circumstances, the capacity of human beings to be inhuman to one another is practically unlimited. Only when the nature of the political problems are addressed can solutions, if they exist, be sought. Despite its undoubted achievements, these are the unpalatable truths that too little television drama over the years set out to probe.

NOTES

1. For a discussion of these advertisements, see Martin McLoone, 'The Commitments – The NIO Confidential Telephone Advertisements', *Fortnight*, no.321, October, 1993, pp.34-6.
2. See, for example, Sarah Dunant, 'The Troubles shooters', *The Guardian*, 20 September, 1993 and Rachell Murrell, '"Screenplay" grasps the Belfast nettle', *The Observer*, 19 September, 1993.
3. Quoted in Fergus Pyle, 'Protests at BBC film on murders in North', *The Irish Times*, 27 January 1989.
4. Bennett explains the problems which his film tries to counteract in Ronan Bennett, 'The Bomber Next Door', *The Guardian*, 23 November, 1992.
5. For the more recent studies, see David Miller, *Don't Mention the War* (London: Pluto Press, 1994) and David Butler, *The Trouble with Reporting Northern Ireland* (Aldershot: Avebury, 1995).
6. *Television Today*, 27 November, 1980, p.18.
7. John Hill, 'Hidden Agenda: Politics and the Thriller', *Circa*, no. 57, 1991, pp.36-41.
8. For a contemporary discussion of the controversy and a reprint of the original and re-edited versions of the prologue, see '"Willie" – Castration or "Common Sense"?', *Broadcast*, 28 August, 1978, pp.3-4.

9. *Television Times*, 5 May, 1983.
10. Quoted in *Television Today*, 26 November, 1981.
11. For a discussion of these issues, see John Hill and Martin McLoone (eds.), *Big Picture, Small Screen: The Relations Between Film and Television* (London: John Libbey, 1996).
12. Quoted in *Television Today*, 16 July, 1987.
13. For an analysis of this, see David Butler, *The Trouble With Reporting Northern Ireland*, especially pp.19-91.
14. John Caughie, 'Progressive Television and Documentary Drama', *Screen*, vol.21. no.3. 1980, pp.9-35.
15. Eamonn McCann and Graham Reid, 'Drama Out of a Crisis', *Broadcast*, 9 September, 1988, pp.17-19.
16. ibid., pp.17-18.
17. ibid., pp.18-19.
18. Paul Clements, 'Four Days in July (Mike Leigh)' in George Brandt (ed.), *British Television Drama in the 1980s* (Cambridge: Cambridge University Press, 1993), pp.163-77.
19. Hazel Holt, 'Avoiding the trap of a documentary style', *Television Today*, 27 March, 1980, p.22.
20. John Wyver, *City Limits*, no.7, 20 November, 1981.
21. Jennifer Lovelace, *Television Today*, 22 February, 1979, p.23.
22. Jill Weekes, *Television Today*, 26 August, 1976, p.13.
23. For an overview of the academic literature on Northern Ireland, see John Whyte, *Interpreting Northern Ireland* (Oxford: Clarendon Press, 1990).

APPENDIX

BBC TELEVISION DRAMA ABOUT NORTHERN IRELAND AND BBC NI TELEVISION DRAMA

The following list is the drama that I know about and does not pretend to be a definite or a comprehensive survey of the field. I have not included episodes of series or serials which have touched on the topic of Northern Ireland. The BBC record should also be seen in the context of a lot of other drama produced over the years by the commercial companies and, especially from the 1980s on, films produced for the cinema which later find their way onto television. I have seen most, but by no means all, of the titles included here and the scarcity of credits for some titles reflects my difficulty in tracking down further information.

1965
Progress to the Park – BBC 2 – tx. 14. 3.65.
(Theatre 625)
Script – Alun Owen.
Dir. – Christopher Morahan.

Cemented With Love – BBC – tx. 5.5.65.
Script – Sam Thompson.
Dir. – M. Leeston-Smith.
Prod. – Peter Luke.

1972
Carson Country – BBC – tx. 23.10.72.
Script – Dominic Behan.
Dir. – Piers Haggard.

1975
The Dandelion Clock – BBC – tx. 15.5.75.
Script – Wilson John Haire.

1976
The Squad – BBC NI – tx. 20.8.76. (30 mins.)
(Centre Play Showcase)
Script – Martin Dillon.
Dir. – John Bruce.

Your Man From the Six Counties – BBC – tx. 26.10.76. (94 mins.)
Script – Colin Welland.
Prod. – Kenith Trodd.
Dir. – Barry Davis.

1977
Catchpenny Twist – BBC NI – tx. 5.12.77.
(Play For Today).
Script – Stewart Parker.
Dir. – Robert Knights.

1978
The Legion Hall Bombing – BBC – tx. 22.8.78.(90 mins).
(Play For Today)
Transcript edited by Caryl Churchill.
Prod. – Margaret Matheson.
Dir. – Roland Joffé.

The Vanishing Army – BBC tx. 29.11.78.
Script – Robert Holles.

The Out of Town Boys – BBC tx. 78.
Script – Ron Hutchinson.

1979
The Last Window Cleaner – BBC – tx. 13.2.79
(Play For Today)
Script – Ron Hutchinson.
Prod. – Kenith Trodd.
Dir. – Bill Craske.

1980
Bought and Sold – BBC NI – tx.28.2.80.
Script – David Hammond.
Dir. – Bill Miskelly.
Music – Paul Brady.

Rifleman – BBC 2 – tx. 27.10.80.(30 mins).
(Première 4).
Script – Maurice Leitch.
Dir. – David Gillard.

Shadows on our Skins – BBC – tx. 20.3.80.(80 mins.)
(Play For Today)
Script – Derek Mahon.
Adapted from novel by Jennifer Johnston.
Prod. – Kenith Trodd.
Dir. – Jim O'Brien.

My Dear Palestrina – BBC NI – tx. 5.12.80.
Script – Bernard MacLaverty.
Prod. – Neil Zeiger.
Dir. – Diarmuid Lawrence.

1981

The Kamikaze Ground Staff Reunion Dinner – BBC – tx.17.2.81.
(Play For Today)
Script – Stewart Parker.
Prod. – Neil Zeiger.
Dir. – Baz Taylor.

Cowboys – BBC NI – tx. 10. 81.(30 mins.)
Script – Harry Towb.
Prod. – Moore Sinnerton.
Dir. – Bill Miskelly.

Iris in the Traffic, Ruby in the Rain – BBC – tx.24.11.81.(65 mins.)
(Play For Today).
Script – Stewart Parker.
Prod. – June Roberts.
Dir. – John Bruce.

1982

Too Late to Talk to Billy – BBC – tx.16.2.82.(85mins.)
(Play For Today).
Script – Graham Reid.
Prods. – Neil Zeiger, Chris Parr.
Dir. – Paul Seed.
(First part of the 'Billy' Plays).

How Many Miles to Babylon? – BBC – tx. 26.2.82. (110 mins.)
(Playhouse)
Script – Derek Mahon.
Adapted from story by Jennifer Johnston.
Prod. – Innes Lloyd.
Dir. Moira Armstrong.

Easter 2016 – BBC – tx. May 82.
Script – Graham Reid.
Prod. – Neil Zeiger.
Dir. – Ben Bolt.

Billy Boy – BBC – tx. Nov.82.
Script – Samantha Lee.
Prod. – Angela Beeching.
Dir. – Christine Secombe.
(Children's play).

Phonefun Limited – BBC – tx.6.7.82.
Script – Bernard MacLaverty.
Prod. – Chris Parr.
Dir. – Bill Miskelly.

1983
Gates of Gold – BBC -tx. 8.3.83.(70mins.)
(Play For Today).
Script – Maurice Leitch.
Prod. – Andreé Molyneaux.
Dir. – Jon Amiel.

Guests of the Nation – BBC – tx. 15.4.83.
Script – Maurice Leitch (from F. O'Connor short story).
Prod. – Andreé Molyneaux.
Dir. – Donald McWhinnie.

A Matter of Choice for Billy – BBC – tx. 10.5.83
Script – Graham Reid.
Prods. – Neil Zeiger, Chris Parr.
Dir. – Paul Seed.
(Second part of the 'Billy' Plays).

Across the Water – BBC – tx. June 83. (75 mins.)
Script – David Rudkin.
Prod. – Kenith Trodd.
Dir. – Paul Seed.

One of Ourselves – BBC – 22.11.83. (50 mins.)
Script – William Trevor.
Prod. – Kenith Trodd.
Dir. – Pat O'Connor.

1984
A Coming to Terms For Billy – BBC NI – tx.21.2.84. (85mins.)
(Play For Today).
Script – Graham Reid.
Prod. – Chris Parr.
Dir. – Paul Seed.
(Third part of the 'Billy' Plays).

A Woman Calling – BBC – tx. 18.4.84.
Script – Anne Devlin.
Prod. – Chris Parr.
Dir. – Sarah Pia Anderson.
(In 1985, won the Samuel Beckett Award for best first play
    for television).

After You've Gone – BBC – tx. 9.5.84.
Script – Frederick Aicken.
Prod. – Chris Parr.
Dir. – Garth Tucker.

Fire At Magilligan – BBC NI – tx. 27.6.84. (45mins.).
Script – Harry Barton.
Prod. – Chris Parr.
Dir. – Jan Sargent.

The Cry – BBC – tx. 31.7.84.
Script – John Montague.
Prod. – Chris Parr.
Dir. – Chris Menaul.

The Long March – BBC NI – tx. 20.11.84.
Script – Anne Devlin.
Prod. – Keith Williams.
Dir. – Chris Parr.

Aunt Suzanne – BBC – tx. 4.1.84.
Script – Michael MacLaverty.
Adapted – Stewart Love.
Prod. – Chris Parr.
Dir. – Peter Barber-Fleming.

1985
Contact – BBC – tx. 6.1.85.
(Screen Two).
Script – AFN Clarke.
Prod. – Terry Coles.
Dir. – Alan Clarke.

We'll Support You Evermore – BBC tx. 14.7.85.
Script – Doug Livingstone.
Prod. – Brenda Reid.
Dir. – Doug Livingstone.

Radio Pictures – BBC – tx. 16.7.85 (55 mins.)
Script – Stewart Parker.
Prod. – Rosemary Hill.
Dir. – Nicholas Renton.

A Night of the Campaign – BBC – tx.4.8.85. (65 mins.).
Script – Robert Glendinning, Leonard Kingston.
Prod. – Andreé Molyneaux.
Dir. – Peter Ormond.

Ties of Blood – BBC – tx. 12.11 – 17.12.85.
   (6/60 mins.)
Script – Graham Reid.
Ex. Prod. – Keith Williams
Prod. – Tim Ironside-Wood.
Dir. – James Ormerod.
(Play titles: McCabe's Wall; Out of Tune; Going Home;
   Attachments; Invitation to a Party; The MilitaryWing).

1986
Four Days in July – BBC -tx. 29.1.86.
Prod. – Kenith Trodd.
Devised and directed – Mike Leigh.

The Daily Woman – BBC tx. 10.8.86.
Script – Bernard MacLaverty.
Prod. – Chris Parr.
Dir. – Martyn Friend.

1987

Naming the Names – BBC Midlands – tx. 8.2.87.(85 mins.).
(Screen Two).
Script – Ann Devlin.
Prod. – Chris Parr.
Dir. – Stuart Burge.

Foreign Bodies – BBC NI – tx. 5.3.87 – 8. 6.89. (Three series).
   (18/30mins.)
Script – Bernard Farrell, Graham Reid.
Prod. – Sydney Lotterby.
Dir. – Sydney Lotterby.

Lorna – BBC NI – tx. 2.6.87.
Script – Graham Reid.
Ex. Prod. – Keith Williams.
Dir. – James Ormerod.
(Follow up play to the 'Billy' trilogy).

Scout – BBC NI – tx. 8.9.87. (60mins.)
(Series title: Next).
Script – Frank McGuinness.
Prod. – Danny Boyle.
Dir. – Danny Boyle.

The Venus De Milo Instead – BBC NI – tx. 9.9.87.(60mins.)
(Series title: Next).
Script – Anne Devlin.
Prod. – Danny Boyle.
Dir. – Danny Boyle

The Rockingham Shoot – BBC NI – tx.10.9.87.(60mins.)
(Series title: Next).
Script – John McGahern.
Prod. – Danny Boyle.
Dir. – Kieran Hickey.

1988
Final Run – BBC – tx. 10.7. – 31.7.88.
   (4/50 mins.)
Script – Carol Bunyan, Ron Hutchinson.
Prod. – Brenda Reid.
Dir. – Tim King.

Crossfire – BBC – tx. 1988 (5 episodes)
Script – John McNeil.
Prod. – Ron Craddock.
Dir. – Ken Hannam.

Tribes – BBC NI tx. 88.(3 parts)
Script – Marie Jones.
Dir. – Henry Laverty.

1989
Elephant – BBC NI – tx. Jan. 89.
Prod. – Danny Boyle.
Dir. – Alan Clarke.

The Nightwatch – BBC NI – tx. Jan. 89.
Script – Ray Brennan.
Prod. – Danny Boyle.
Dir. – Danny Boyle.

Monkeys – BBC NI – tx. Jan. 89.
Script – Paul Muldoon.
Prod. – Danny Boyle.
Dir. – Danny Boyle.

Chinese Whispers – BBC NI – tx. 2.8.89.(60 mins.)
(Screenplay)
Script – Maurice Leitch.
Prod. – Robert Cooper.
Dir. – Stuart Burge.

Beyond The Pale – BBC NI – tx. 30.8.89.(65 mins.)
(Screenplay).
Script – William Trevor (from his own short story).
Prod. – Robert Cooper.
Dir. – Diarmuid Lawrence.

The Hen House – BBC NI – tx. 6.9.89. (60 mins.).
(Screenplay)
Script – Frank McGuinness.
Prod. – Robert Cooper.
Dir. – Danny Boyle.

1990
Pentecost – BBC – tx. 14.7.90. (85 mins.)
(Theatre Night).
Script – Stewart Parker.
Adapted – Lesley Bruce.
Dir. – Nicholas Kent.

The Englishman's Wife – BBC NI – tx. 1.8.90 (60 mins.)
(Screenplay)
Script – Holly Chandler.
Prod. – Robert Cooper.
Dir. – Robert Cooper.

A Safe House – BBC NI – tx. 22.8.90.(60 mins.)
(Screenplay)
Script – Bill Morrison.
Prod. – Robert Cooper.
Dir. – Moira Armstrong.

August Saturday – BBC NI – tx. 29.12.90.
(Screenplay)
Script – William Trevor.
Prod. – Robert Cooper.
Dir. – Diarmuid Lawrence.

1991
Events At Drimaghleen – BBC NI(with RTE) – tx. 17.7.91.
(Screenplay)
Script – William Trevor (from his own short story).
Prod. – Robert Cooper.
Dir. – Robert Cooper.

Murder in Eden – BBC NI – tx.19.7.-2.8.91. (3 episodes).
Script – Shane Connaughton (adapted from 'Bogmail' by
Patrick McGinley.)
Prod. – Robert Cooper.
Dir. – Nicholas Renton.

Arise and Go Now BBC – tx. 8.91
(Screen Play)
Script – Owen O'Neill.
Producer – Paul Lister.
Dir. – Danny Boyle.

So You Think You've Got Troubles – Alomo Prods. for BBC –
tx.17.10.-28.11.91.(6/30 episodes).
Script – Laurence Marks, Maurice Gran.
Ex. Prods. – Allan McKeown, Michael Pilswort.
Prod. – Tara Prem.
Dir. – Colm Villa, Mike Holgate.

Children of the North – BBC – tx.30.10.-20.11.91 (4 episodes).
Script – John Hale (adapted from the trilogy by MS Power).
Prod. Chris Parr.
Dir. – David Drury.
(Episode titles: The Killing of Yesterday's Children; Lonely the
   Men Without Heroes; City of Moloch; A Darkness in the Eye).

1992
Force of Duty – RTE with BBC NI – tx. 8.7.92.(80.5 mins.)
(Screenplay)
Script – Bill Morrison, Chris Ryder.
Prod. – Robert Cooper.
Dir. – Pat O'Connor.

You, Me and Marley – BBC NI – tx. 30.9.92. (84 mins. 16mm.)
(Screenplay)
Script – Graham Reid.
Prod. Chris Parr.
Dir. – Richard Spence.

1993
Love Lies Bleeding – BBC NI (with Télécip) – tx. 22.9.93 (86 mins.)
(Screenplay)
Script – Ronan Bennett.
Prod. – Robert Cooper.
Dir. – Michael Winterbottom.

The Railway Station Man – BBC – tx. 11.93.
(Screen Two)
Script – Shelagh Delaney (from the novel by
Jennifer Johnston).
Ex. Prods. – Lauren Joy Sand, Mark Shivas.
Prod. – Roger Randall-Cutler.
Dir. – Michael Whyte.

1994
All Things Bright and Beautiful – Good Film Company
(for BBC NI and BSE) – tx.16.3.94. (90 mins.)
(Screen Two)
Script – Barry Devlin.
Ex. Prods. – Robert Cooper, Paul McGuinness, Mark Shivas.
Prod. – Katy McGuinness.
Dir. – Barry Devlin.

O Mary This London – BBC – tx.30.3.94. (90 mins.)
(Screen Two)
Script – Shane Connaughton.
Ex. Prod. – Mark Shivas.
Prod. – Helen Greaves.
Dir. – Suri Krishnamma.

Henri – BBC NI (with RTE) tx. 20.4.94. (59 mins.)
(Screen Two)
Script – John Forte.
Ex. Prod. – Robert Cooper, George Faber.
Prod. – Colin Tucker.
Dir. – Simon Shore.

A Breed of Heroes – BBC NI – tx. 9.94.
Script – Charles Wood.

1995
Life After Life – BBC NI – tx. 4. 95.
(Screen Two)
Script – Graham Reid.
Prod. – Anthony Rowe.
Dir. – Tim Fywell.

The Hanging Gale – BBC NI – tx. 4. 95 (4 parts).
Script – Allan Cubitt.
Prod. – Jonathan Cavendish.
Dir. – Diarmuid Lawrence.

Runway One – BBC NI – tx. 9.95.
Script – Barry Devlin.
Prod. – Robert Cooper.
Dir. – David Drury.

A Man of No Importance (for the cinema) – BBC NI.
Script – Barry Devlin.
Dir. – Suri Krishnamma.

Ballykissangel – BBC NI – tx. 11.2 – 17.3.96 (6 parts).
Script – Kieran Prendiville.
Prod. – Joy Lale.
Dir. – Paul Harrison.

THE MEDIA AND NORTHERN IRELAND
SOME PERSONAL RECOLLECTIONS, 1969-80

Keith Kyle

I was never directly connected with the Northern Ireland region
of the BBC, but was instead one of those who was 'parachuted in'
by the BBC in 1969, in my case on behalf of the *Tonight* programme, in response to the drastic increase of national interest
created by the events at Burntollet Bridge in January of that year.
Off and on, I kept returning to the province until 1980. *Tonight*, it
may be recalled, was a daily current affairs programme on
Channel 1, fulfilling some of the same functions that are nowadays
fulfilled by *Newsnight*. I did not arrive on the scene entirely raw, as
I had been in Ireland a decade before on behalf of *The Economist*,
whose political and parliamentary correspondent I then was, and
had been exposed at that time to the highly specialised nature of
Northern Ireland politics and to some, at least, of the characteristics of Northern Ireland politicians. Moreover, out of personal
interest, I had, in the year just before the Troubles started, been
reading quite extensively in recent Irish history, including that of
the North.

Nevertheless, to come to Northern Ireland at that particular
time was to experience quite a shock. Having been a foreign correspondent in the United States during the civil rights' movement, in Africa and in the Middle East, I was hardly a stranger to
political breakdown and civil strife. Yet this had always been a matter of reporting from abroad, of seeking to convey to a British
audience the elements of a situation that was exotic; now a comparable situation was occurring *at home*, but in a setting with which
the vast bulk of the audience could not be expected to identify
instinctively as a domestic one. Some of the actions displayed and
opinions expressed must, indeed, have appeared to people on the
mainland as coming from the dark side of the moon.

It was going to be no easy task to explain how a *domestic* political crisis in a part of the United Kingdom in the mid-twentieth century could involve the extensive use of violence, the burning of houses, the expression of political views in vehemently sectarian terms. On the one hand, it was necessary to ensure that British people felt it was their crisis, not someone else's that they were looking in at; if they were to take it seriously they must sample the depth and intensity of the passions involved. Yet at the same time we were going to have to bear in mind that what was transmitted nationally could be received locally, what we said and what we showed could directly affect the course of events.

Much had changed in the ten years since I had last been in Northern Ireland. At that time, with certain exceptions (the abstentionists on the one side and the Northern Ireland Labour Party in a few urban constituencies on the other) the rule was followed that the Unionist Party should not be challenged by Protestants in Protestant majority areas and that the Nationalist Party should not be challenged by Catholics in Catholic majority areas. This made each election to parliament at Stormont in effect a referendum on the continuation of partition. Among nationalists elected, their behaviour towards the local parliament, a body whose legitimacy they did not respect, was ambivalent at best. Their policy towards it is described by the historian of Ulster, Jonathan Bardon, as 'one of intermittent and erratic abstentionism.'[1]

Now, ten years later, the Unionist monopoly among Protestants was being everywhere challenged by Dr. Ian Paisley and his Democratic Unionists and the nationalist monopoly was being challenged by new, young, in many cases university-based politicians who formed the People's Democracy – the PDs – and called for the abandonment of the standard, sterile, North of Ireland duopoly. Rallies were being held and processions formed by Civil Rights movements and various socialist bodies protesting against unemployment and bad housing. These movements proclaimed themselves to be non-sectarian and to a limited extent they were, though their numbers were drawn disproportionately from the Catholic community. Rather demonstratively they were not, however, talking about the border. The civil rights demonstrations were demanding full *British* rights, such as ending the system of gerrymandering of local government constituencies and the unfair allocation of jobs and housing and other resources on the basis of religion. It was of the essence of these New Politics that an effort was always made to avoid any sectarian symbols.

I first encountered this climate when I entered 'Free Derry', as the people of the Creggan and the Bogside termed the autonomous area which had been proclaimed in the nationalist sections of Londonderry, a city in which the gerrymandering was most blatant. It was typical – a point which I made in my television report – that, when it was seen that someone had raised the tri-colour flag of the Irish Republic, it was a well-known IRA veteran who was sent to pull it down. Free Derry was very anxious to make it known that this was a new kind of battle.

In Belfast, some Protestants, in revenge presumably for the demonstrations which they regarded as sectarian and directed against them, began burning down the houses of Catholics. There were also huge Unionist demonstrations. Very soon after I had reached Belfast, I arranged with the late John McQuade, a docker who had become a Unionist MP at Stormont, to spend an evening in his sitting room in the Shankill Road with a bunch of his neigh-bours. The language of bitterness and hatred with which they characterised the nationalist population was comparable only to things that I had heard said about the blacks in the American South. I once asked Mr McQuade on camera why he was demand-ing that Catholic families be moved out of the Unity flats, a block which had been consciously designed to foster integrated living. McQuade replied, 'My idea is that they are saying they are antag-onised by our parades. If they were moved back they would not see our colours. . . Our colours, as I say and shall maintain, are not kicking the Pope but are shown to us and our children as the vic-tory of good over evil, of King William over King James.' In few places elsewhere in the world, I think, is a historical event three hundred years before kept perpetually in the people's eye as hav-ing happened only yesterday in the way that the Battle of the Boyne is represented in the graffiti and processions of Northern Ireland. Perhaps the Battle of Kossovo is the nearest comparitor, but in this case what is commemorated by the Serbs is a cata-strophic defeat; in Northern Ireland the anniversary of the Boyne is for Unionists a triumphalist occasion.

The atmosphere at Broadcasting House, on the corner of Ormeau and Linenhall Streets, in the whorl of demonstration and counter-demonstration, was understandably tense; the local broadcasters, drawn from both communities, plus of course, the ever-increasing numbers of us invaders, found themselves directly involved in the constantly shifting street scenes. If I may quote from something which I wrote at the time, which was republished in a book called *A Listener Anthology* edited by Karl Miller, 'It was a climate of anger, anguish, reproach and deputation in which every new bulletin and current affairs programme produced a minimum of 40 to 50 telephone calls and each brought into the building its quota of overwrought citizens exercising their privilege of shouting at the BBC in person.'[2]

People who had regarded the BBC all their lives as a reliable part of the Ulster establishment considered that our readiness to entertain a concept of impartiality as between the 'loyal' and the 'disloyal' was an odious betrayal. For some, the very appearance on the screen of the Republican Labour MP Gerry Fitt and the Civil rights spokesman John Hume was a unforgivable lapse from grace. 'Even before the fighting started,' I wrote in 1969, 'there was a widespread view among the Unionists that the BBC was neutral against them.'

A sustained Civil Rights campaign, as journalists who, like myself, had covered the American civil rights movement were aware, presents responsible television with very special problems. To quote again from the chapter in *A Listener Anthology*, in a passage in which I attempted at the time to examine the characteristics of a non-violent campaign and how these interact with the media by which it is reported, 'The leaders of the campaign must be able to discipline their followers [to exercise restraint while at the same time making] credible the danger of violence. . . Moreover if the forces in possession are sufficiently provoked by a non-violent campaign to resort to violence and if this is done in the public eye, the non-violent protester will have won a major victory. The concept of violence, its incipiency on one side or the other, is therefore an absolutely indispensable part of the technique of non-violence.' In view of this, my article went on, 'it becomes exceedingly difficult for television to be both impartial and responsible, two ideals that usually run together. . . Television is a valuable instrument for the non-violent campaigner. He needs it to provoke – perhaps by exposing the truth – and so cause the tension to escalate. To what extent should television let itself be manipulated to escalate tension?' One should always remember that, unlike a print journalist with his notebook or even without one, television is a very visible presence on the scene.

This may give some indication of the kind of issues which both-ered reporters, many of whom had spent their time exposing other people's dirty linen and were suddenly confronted with dirty linen on home ground. At that stage the IRA were seldom to be seen, except in the graffiti of the Roman Catholic streets making the equation: 'IRA=I Ran Away.' Old IRA members were present at civil rights demonstrations (I had individual members pointed out to me) but they were not prominent and kept to their low profile even when the fighting first broke out. The element of extremism was rather on the other side, in the sulphurous, anti-Roman sermons being preached by Dr. Ian Paisley. In mid-August 1969, the situation in Belfast was one in which live coverage in BBC news bulletins of street scenes of crude abuse and total disorder would, in a flash, empty the nearby pubs of the side being abused as men poured out to take part in the fight. At this point the BBC imposed a measure of self-censorship.

At a special meeting in the Director-General's office on the third day of the disorders, and before the British troops actually arrived, the Corporation decided on what was termed 'a temporary departure from normal journalistic considerations.' What was happening was to be explained but not shown. Street interviews, in which members of the public were given to expressing themselves in the most extreme way, were temporarily banned; and two individuals in particular, Ian Paisley and Bernadette Devlin, were to be kept off the screen. Personally I felt it was wrong to have any censorship for the whole network, especially if British people were going to understand the need to send in troops to keep order in our own country. Accordingly, I suggested that bans like those on Devlin and Paisley should only apply to the region and not to the rest of the country. The BBC's view was that their programmes must be a seamless weave. One should not play down in Belfast what one was putting out elsewhere; otherwise the integrity of the service would be in question. The bans on Paisley and Devlin were soon lifted and, though there were subsequent problems about coverage, my worst fears about the precedents that were being set were not realised.

At a later date, after the Provisionals had split off from the more restrained Official IRA – a split whose sinister significance was first identified on the BBC by a young activist in the people's Democracy, now Professor Kevin Boyle – television journalists were constantly complaining about what they called the BBC's ban on interviewing the IRA. There was at that time a tendency among

media critics to reproach the BBC with being too responsive to the
requirements of the security forces, and within the BBC there was
a feeling among programme-makers that their own hierarchy was
not sufficiently protective of their independence as journalists.
There were occasions, as I shall illustrate, when I momentarily
came to share this view. But taking the period of the Troubles as a
whole I would conclude that the BBC has come out of it pretty
well.

In the matter of the so-called IRA ban, I pointed out that the
small-print of the BBC management's decree did not say that
there should be no interviews at all but it did say that anyone
proposing an IRA interview should have to get the Director-
Generals' personal permission. I was told by some of my colleagues that that was as good as a ban but, despite the general
scepticism, I put forward a reasoned case and was granted permission. The interview took place in the Republic. It didn't cause the
BBC serious trouble. The Provisional Sinn Féin had at this time a
fancy scheme for the political reorganisation of a united Ireland.
The four original provinces, of which a nine-county Ulster is one,
would be re-constituted and most governmental powers would be
devolved to them. Moreover, in the case of Ulster, there would be
much further devolution into the East and West region separated
by the Bann. Ruairi O Bradaigh, the Sinn Féin leader of the day,
Gerry Adams's predecessor, outlined this in considerable detail,
answering every objection with the bland assurance that once the
principle of the plan was adopted all would be transformed. The
IRA/Sinn Féin have appeared since to have dropped that particular constitutional solution.[3]

With the pouring in of one after another of the production
teams from the major current affairs programmes, there was, I
suppose, bound to be some friction with a BBC Controller,
Northern Ireland, who was accustomed to run his own patch and
who, it should in all fairness be stated, had to live with the local
consequences of these outside commentaries on Ulster's affairs. It
should also be stated that, on the evidence of those who worked in
the Belfast newsroom, the first Regional Controller whom I
encountered and with whom I eventually came into collision,
Waldo Maguire, was regarded as 'a breathe of fresh air' when he
arrived from London, where he had edited television news.
Maguire was himself an Ulsterman, a genial if somewhat intense
individual and a mine of information about the Province, which

he generously shared. And he was certainly no admirer of the traditional style of Ulster politics. I found him normally co-operative and always realised that he was working under great strain and, for a while, with inadequate resources.

In 1971, I was making a feature on Northern Ireland politics. I had reached the conclusion that, despite the modernising tendency currently represented by Brian Faulkner, who made a substantial appearance in my film and was indeed allowed the last word, the support for old-fashioned Unionism, symbolised by the marches and ceremonies of the Orange Order, remained stronger than some people thought. Moreover I also felt that the Chichester-Clark Government at Stormont was very fragile and was unlikely to last. These judgements, though not stated so baldly as here, were no doubt implicit in the balance of the report.

Under the rules prevailing, I left a copy of the film with the Regional Controller, who had a right of veto over anything coming from the region, and departed for the Republic to make my next film. I then discovered by phone that Mr Maguire had in fact put a stopper on my report. His reason was that, first, he was convinced that the modernisers had the public behind them and that traditional Unionism was rapidly dying out; second, even if this proved not to be so and the Government did fall, he did not want it to be said that the BBC had contributed to that result. 'It wouldn't be so bad,' he told me, 'if you were shown standing in a field and speaking the whole commentary as a personal view into camera.' That was not however how current affairs items in the early Seventies were made. I immediately appealed to the Director-General; eventually the BBC ruled in my favour, but by then the question was moot. The Chichester-Clark Government had fallen; the programme was too dated to transmit.

In March 1973 the next Prime Minister, Brian Faulkner, was interviewed in a programme called *A Question of Ulster* by a panel of interviewers in the BBC's London studios, with a retired senior judge, Lord Devlin in the chair. Ideas about new political institutions were in the air and the British Government was about to produce a White Paper. From the time of my first few weeks in Northern Ireland in 1969 I had been convinced that the normal Westminster form of democracy would not work in the province because normal party life and normal party elections did not exist there. What I thought was needed was some way of producing what I called then a 'compulsory coalition'; since the Sunningdale conference it has been known by the more user-friendly term of a power-sharing executive.

In the programme Faulkner outlined his ideas for giving unprecedented powers to committees of the legislature, many of which could be chaired by the opposition. But when I questioned him about the Cabinet and whether he would agree to have Gerry Fitt and John Hume as fellow-Ministers, he dug in his heels. He clearly thought his party could not take Cabinet Ministers whose allegiance to the Union was ambiguous. Before the programme went out, the British Government had leaned on the BBC quite hard to cancel it completely because they had been genuinely worried that someone would ask the question that I did in fact ask, whereupon Faulkner might paint himself into a corner, as indeed he seemed to do. I saw the point but I did not believe that a broadcaster could allow himself to become an arm of the government to this extent. In any event, despite what he said on the BBC, Faulkner did in the end agree to have Fitt and Hume as Ministers. A majority in the Ulster Unionist Council repudiated him; the power-sharing regime lasted about four months. The fact that Faulkner had made so public a U-turn on so major a point was one of the missiles that were hurled against him.

The most controversial programme with which I was associated in Ireland was the Bernard O'Connor interview. Bernard O'Connor was a school teacher and driving instructor in Enniskillen. He is an outspoken Republican and in 1969 at the time of the early civil rights agitation when he was an active member of the People's Democracy, he ran a small, rather cheeky magazine which had offended members of the local power elite in Fermanagh, Catholic as well as Protestant. He also – which is of crucial importance to this story – has remarkable powers of total recall. I had not gone to Enniskillen in 1977 with the purpose of meeting him. On the contrary I was going on a rather low-key story about the new local councils. In intervals of filming the Fermanagh Council in action, I was persistently lobbied by one of its SDLP members to talk to a man who had been discharged by the police after undergoing interrogation at the Castlereagh barracks. I was in a hurry, I was not investigating the RUC, and was very leery of allegations which, up to then, seemed to come exclusively from Sinn Féin. The councillor was importunate, and I agreed to see his man for a few minutes.

My initial impression of O'Connor was favourable and I immediately realised that he would make a natural for television: precise, coherent, fluent, intelligible. That meant that if the BBC put him on the screen, he would probably carry conviction; to me that made the responsibility involved in putting him on at all that much greater. Moreover, I had a great deal of sympathy for the predicament of the RUC. I had not had a long enough conversation with O'Connor to reach any conclusion and, in any case, the final decision would not be mine. When we returned to London, my producer, Janine Thomason, recommended to the editor of Tonight that we take up the story and after some initial hesitation this was tentatively agreed. I was sent back without a crew to make further enquiries. Janine and I spent altogether seven hours with O'Connor and a great deal more with people who could throw light on his personality, background, and activities. It seemed established that he was not connected with Sinn Féin or any other political party since his days with the PDs. He had been detained on suspicion of being a 'godfather' of the IRA but after a week's interrogation at Castlereagh they had had to release him (and, I may say, nothing has been found against him since). He insisted that he enjoyed good relations with members of the uniformed police and that he had nothing against them, though he did admit that in the early, hectic days of peaceful demonstration, when the only violence came from the other side, he had once said, 'The only good policeman is a dead policeman.'

Bernard O'Connor's interrogation, by his own account, was in every respect abusive – immensely long overnight sessions without a break, interrogation while obliged to undress and to be subjected to various forms of acute physical stress, punching in the ribs, demeaning physical acts, endless insults relating to his religion and his family and threats, such as that if he were released it would be onto the Shankill Road with the UVF alerted as to when he would be there. It immediately struck me that the acts described appeared to coincide with the lesser of the two categories of 'inhuman and degrading treatment' in respect of which the British Government had been found guilty by the European Human Rights Commission at Strasbourg. As it happened, when driving to Enniskillen, before we had spoken to O'Connor, Janine and I had heard on the car radio that the Attorney-General, Sam Silkin, had given Britain's word that all acts complained of by the Irish Government (which has brought the Strasbourg case) had been completely ended, that there was no question of recurrence, and that, therefore, Britain should be let off the final stage of a Strasbourg case, prosecution before the Human Rights Court.

Informally I laid the details of O'Connor's allegations before the late Sir James Fawcett, then the chairman of the European Human Rights Commission, and he confirmed to me that he would consider the case, if shown to be genuine, as falling directly under the rubric of cruel, inhuman and degrading treatment. It was this, really, that made me feel that it was right to proceed with a television film.

I decided that the really remarkable thing about O'Connor's testimony was its meticulous completeness; he had the gift of total recall; he had his interrogations precisely timed (he said he was able to read a wristwatch upside down); the appearance, dress and mood of each interrogator were exactly detailed; the sequence of exchanges between him and each interrogator was vividly laid out. It was apparent that if an accurate impression were to be given of his story that he should have much more time than a usual *Tonight* item and that his presence and manner were sufficient to hold the attention of an audience for a longer period. The Editor of *Tonight* sent Janine Thomason and me with a crew to interview O'Connor, without any guarantee of subsequent transmission and we came back with over an hour of material.

I recommended that the Director-General's permission be sought – this was not technically essential because no one had suggested that O'Connor was literally a member of the IRA (and he expressed disapproval of its violent methods) but I was pretty certain that we should run into some political trouble and I thought that if the D-G was going to be in at the crash landing it was only fair to him that he should be there at the takeoff. He appointed two very senior figures, both now dead, one of them the late Sir Richard Francis, who was by now the Belfast Region Controller, to see the film and advise him. When they had seen it, they told me that they believed that Bernard O'Connor was telling the truth. They said, however, that transmission should be postponed a fortnight to give the Chief Constable of the RUC more notice and to give me a chance to go back to Enniskillen and to put on film some of the surrounding research I had got in my notebook, including an interview with O'Connor's doctor who had examined him while in detention and had found worrying traces of ill-treatment and also a short interview with another man who had complained against the police. In return I could have the full hour of

Tonight, which could include up to 40 minutes of my interview of O'Connor. When I returned to Enniskillen I found the nationalist community confirmed in its suspicion that the BBC would never be allowed (or, perhaps, want) to put out this programme. The credibility of the BBC's claim to be impartial as between the two communities was visibly at stake.

In the event, the RUC declined to comment except for a one line statement, to which we, of course, give full prominence. I had been asked to make an introductory statement – I used this to emphasise the grave nature of the security situation and the perilous task of the RUC, but I also laid out the facts of the European Commission's finding and the Attorney-General's speech.

All hell broke loose the following day; the BBC was under intense attack in the tabloids, the cartoonists had a field day, one ('Jak' in the *Evening Standard*) showing a man spreadeagled on the pavement and a BBC reporter, not, I was glad to note, looking particularly like me, offering a microphone to masked gunmen, bristling with machine-guns and inviting their opinion. Even *The Times*, in a leader which generally rebutted the wider criticisms of the BBC's coverage of Northern Ireland, defined the issues raised by the O'Connor interviews very fairly, only to come down on balance against the showing of it. The day afterwards was to be the regular meeting of the BBC Board of Governors and, at the Director-General's request, Ms Thomason and I stayed up all night preparing a detailed report on every stage of our actions. Fortunately the Governors backed without reservation the decision to transmit.

Reactions in the Province can be guessed: favourable comment in the *Irish News* and by civil rights activists and the SDLP; bitter resentment by spokesmen of the Unionists and the RUC. The Vanguard Unionist party expressed its 'utter revulsion' at the programme and went on, 'Amazement is the only description one can give to the fantastic memory of the alleged victim, who despite his terrible suffering was able to memorise every single event including the actual length of each happening. How gullible does the BBC think the public are?' An RUC spokesman was quoted in the press as saying that, 'The fear here is that terrorists might seize on this as provocation to kill more policemen.'

At the time of the O'Connor interview 99 Ulster police had been murdered since the Provo violence had begun. Eleven days after the interview, 18 year old Police Constable William Brown was killed by the IRA in Fermanagh: the Provos' statement sought to link this with the RUC having been 'shown to the world as the torture instrument of the British war machine.' This translated into a banner headline, 'MURDER BY TV; BBC accused after assassination' on the front page of the *Daily Express.* The chairman of the Ulster Police Federation was quoted as saying that the *Tonight* programme had borne the hallmarks of trial by TV. In the House of Lords, Viscount Brookborough, son of the late Prime Minster of Northern Ireland, demanded to know 'At what stage does a part of the State establishment provide the IRA with a platform on which to put their view?' The BBC kept cool under the pressure; the Director-General, Sir Charles Curran, said that the IRA needed no fresh excuse for killing members of the security forces.

The Attorney-General sent for me. He had read the script of the film and was in obvious distress at the apparent breach of his pledge to the Council of Europe. There was an official procedure for complaints against the police and O'Connor had filed such a complaint. As with many previous cases the Director of Public Prosecutions had decided that there was insufficient evidence for action to be taken against the police officers at Castlereagh. But the Attorney-General took pains to explain to me the advantages to a person in O'Connor's position of going to court with a civil suit against the Chief Constable of the RUC, since the standards of proof required of the plaintiff are not so exacting as those required for a criminal prosecution – 'beyond reasonable doubt' for the latter but only 'balance of probabilities' in a civil case. Silkin did this in a way which made me feel that he was as good as offering his legal advice to O'Connor to press the suit. O'Connor was in any case inclined to sue.

I was extremely interested in the result. I had done my best to test O'Connor's *bona fides* but I am not a lawyer and this was the first time he would be publicly examined by lawyers. The legal process known as 'discovery' revealed the identities and time cards of O'Connor's various interrogators, showing the extraordinary accuracy of his account on television. Some of his allegations of the application of violence were thought by Mr Justice Murray to be exaggerated. Notwithstanding this, on 30 June 1980, more than three years after his ordeal, Bernard O'Connor was awarded exemplary damages.[4]

It should not be thought that every one of the many reports

from Ireland which I made at various intervals throughout the Seventies up until my *Two Traditions in Ireland* in 1980 were occasions for controversy. Quite the contrary in fact, they usually were not. I have simply picked out instances which may cast some light on the issues confronting the media when disorder strikes close to home.

NOTES

1. Jonathan Bardon, *A History of Ulster* (Belfast: Blackstaff Press, 1992), pp.511-12. For impressions of Northern Ireland politics in 1959 see Keith Kyle (1959) 'Irish Notebook – I', *The Economist* p.941, 19 September and 'Irish Notebook – II' p1035, 26 September; 'Ulster Variations', *The Economist*, p.1004, 26, September; 'Ulster Opportunities', *The Economist* p. 222, 17 October.
2. Keith Kyle, 'Ulster and the BBC' in Karl Miller (ed.), *A Listener Anthology, August 1967-June 1970* (London: BBC, 1970) pp. 47-51.
3. Keith Kyle (1972), 'The Provisionals' Regional Plan for a United Ireland,' *The Listener*, 16 March; and 'The Provisionals' Green Paper,' *The Listener*, pp. 3-4, 6 July.
4. The best published account of the O'Connor case is in Peter Taylor, *Beating the Terrorists ? Interrogation at Omagh, Gough and Castlereagh* (Harmondsworth: Penguin, 1980) pp. 162-74. See also, Keith Kyle (1977), 'Bernard O'Connor's Story,' *The Listener*, pp. 101-2, 26 January.

REPORTING THE CONFLICT

Keith Baker

I joined the BBC in 1982 after a long time in newspaper journalism. Indeed, I had been with the *Belfast Telegraph* since the historic year of 1969. But for six highly eventful and very challenging years, I enjoyed what I can only describe as the privilege of being Head of News and Current Affairs for the BBC in Northern Ireland. This paper, then, comes from someone who was very much at the heart of BBC coverage.

Before we go any further, it is perhaps worth pausing for a moment to reflect on where we are and the environment in which the BBC is currently broadcasting.

When I delivered the original text of this paper at a symposium in Coleraine towards the end of 1994, the ceasefires were only a few months old and I reflected then on how much had changed in twelve months. In December 1994, there seemed to be no conflict on which to report and the future, although certainly unclear, had a brighter tinge to it. A year before, the themes would have been very different, with violence very high on the agenda. We were still reeling from the shock waves of the Shankill bombing, the massacre at Greysteel, the murder of the workmen in a council depot in Belfast, all the steady, dripping horror of terrorism and sectarian hatred. That was the year in which, on UTV, the Northern Ireland Office were running advertisements for the confidential telephone to the tune of *In The Bleak Midwinter*. All a very long way from the up-beat message of Van Morrison and Time For The Bright Side.

What was happening on the political front? John Hume and Gerry Adams had come to the end of their discussions and we all wondered what it would lead to, if anything. The Government had been embarrassed by revelations of contact between them and representatives of the IRA and there was a very strong indication that Dublin and London were trying to put together some sort of joint declaration which they wanted to issue before Christmas but there was a lot of doubt as to whether they would be able to resolve their various differences in order to do so.

But the Downing Street Declaration came into being, although differences, at many levels, persisted and grew. What also grew over the last eighteen months was optimism, symbolised at one level by the cars on our streets and the tourists in our hotels and resorts during the glorious summer of 1995, and at another level by events like the Washington economic conference and the outpouring of welcome given to Bill and Hillary Clinton in November.

Then came the bomb at Canary Wharf and those feelings of hope seemed to have been blown to pieces with it. Once again Northern Ireland faces an uncertain future, once again soldiers are on the streets and the police are stopping traffic.

All of which, I think, demonstrates more than amply that we can expect the affairs of Northern Ireland and its ever-changing fortunes to be a source of international political interest and of world news for many years to come. The story continues to unfold and although I write specifically for those who work for the BBC, all journalists who report events here are once more in a period of great challenge as we look ahead uncertainly.

We will come back to the future in a moment or two but first, how have we handled it all so far? When the Troubles began, I was in the editorial department of the *Belfast Telegraph* but I know that experiences there were mirrored in the BBC. Quite simply, when it all blew up, we did not know what was going on.

The BBC newsroom, which, it is probably fair to say, had been a reasonably undemanding patch up until then, was swamped. There was not the staff to cope with what was happening, there was not the experience to handle it, there was not the professional expertise to understand it. Add to that the fact that our actual broadcast output was a mere fraction of what it is now on both radio and television. There was no Radio Ulster, no Radio Foyle. We were not equipped in any way for a story of such magnitude. No-one knew how long it was all going to last and I think there was a genuine fear, fear of somehow misusing the power of what broadcasting we had in a way that might just make things worse.

Martin Bell tells the story of the burning of Farringdon Gardens in 1969 and the mass exodus of refugees from there and how he was instructed from on high within the BBC in Belfast not to report that the victims were Catholics. Now hindsight is a wonderful thing and in the news business important judgements often have to be made on the hoof and while I would disagree with the decision made that day, as Martin describes it, I can understand perfectly the concern that led to it – a concern that what the BBC was broadcasting should not fan the flames any higher.

There are still echoes of that today. Not long ago, I was introduced to someone who remarked, when they heard what my job was, 'Oh, so you're responsible for all this trouble?'

But we have learned through experience. We have learned a great deal about our role and our responsibilities within the community through difficult and painful times. We have shared with the people to whom we broadcast all the trauma of the loss of more than 3,000 lives, destruction on a massive scale, a conflict that has seemed to have no end.

There have been some bitter experiences, of course, such as the UWC strike in 1974 and the extraordinary dilemma which that episode presented to a public service broadcaster. In a context such as that, with the authorities to all intents and purposes doing nothing and those not in authority doing everything, what constitutes the public interest, what is the public service role? What should we have told people? Should we have told them about road blocks and where they could get petrol and what state the power stations were in? Or should we have just kept people in the dark, wondering what was happening down the street, whether you could get to work or not? Did the information we provided in effect help to keep the strike going and add legitimacy to it? There are questions about that period which will be discussed eternally, I suspect. And indeed, one point of view on the subject was expressed rather graphically, if not terribly eloquently, a short time after the strike when the IRA set off a car bomb outside our front door.

Then there is Carrickmore and *Real Lives*, programmes not made here by us but which have certainly had a bearing on the role of the BBC within this community. Because we are, after all, the BBC in Northern Ireland, part of the wider BBC and not a self-contained, self-financing private venture.

Go on down the years, through the hunger strikes, Gibraltar, Enniskillen, the Anglo-Irish Agreement and all the loyalist protests which followed it, a particularly difficult time for our reporting staff who were often attacked once the cameras were seen and the letters 'BBC' mentioned.

And I suppose, in many ways, when I joined the BBC, that was the first thing I noticed, that, in spite of our aspiration to be objective, to take neither one side nor the other but to provide focused journalism that was as impartial as it could be, we were seen not as observers somehow but as part of the story itself, often to the delight of our print colleagues for whom we have always been good copy. 'Fury over Beeb film on —' You can insert your own topic because there have been a good many of them down the years.

The reason, of course, is that first letter, 'B', in the organisation's title and I soon discovered that the 'B' for British was a centre of controversy where the 'B' for *Belfast Telegraph* was not.

Perceptions in Northern Ireland can be everything and we have been dogged by them. If I characterise the community here as having two sides, I know that is an over-simplistic way of referring to it, but let us say there are those on one side who see the word British as signifying that we must have a particular point of view, that we cannot be objective, that my daily editorial meetings probably cannot take place until I hear what Stormont has decided should go in our programmes. On the other hand, there are those who quite simply believe that we are just not British enough, that we are broadcasting both people and opinions which should not be heard and that we are really all fellow-travellers with those who would seek to destroy our sovereignty.

Behind both points of view, of course, is the word 'bias'. It is a word with which we are very familiar in the BBC and which is often interchangeable with the word British in some of the letters we receive, often unsigned.

As I said, perceptions can be everything. I went to the Edinburgh Television Festival in August, 1994, where there was a series of sessions entitled 'Getting It Wrong?' in which various speakers were asked to give their perspective on how the media had reported Northern Ireland over the years. Inevitably, of course, it became a debate on how the BBC had reported Northern Ireland over the years.

At one session, Pat McGeown, who is a member of the Sinn Féin executive, said that the BBC here couldn't be expected to present an impartial view because it was all run by people of a Unionist persuasion. At a subsequent session, John Taylor said the Unionist point of view didn't get a proper airing because there were too many people of a Catholic/nationalist background.

So there you are. Who are you to believe? Personally, I would prefer to believe the views of our audiences and in particular the people surveyed for us just a couple of months ago by Ulster Marketing Surveys as part of an exhaustive review which we undertook of our local programme strategy. It was their view that we presented the news unbiased and unadorned and with an impartiality and objectivity which allowed people to judge events and issues for themselves.

That objectivity is something we cherish. And it was something which was dealt a severe blow towards the end of 1988 when the Government introduced the Broadcasting Ban.

May I say that it is a delight to be able to refer to this episode in broadcasting history in the past tense. Of all the obstacles placed in the way of even-handedness, this was the most difficult. The Government, as the then-Controller here, Dr. Colin Morris, put it, had declared impartiality illegal. How could we pursue objectivity in the face of such a road-block? Well, the answer was that the road was not blocked entirely. You could still get through but there was only one lane open. The trick was to ensure that our journalists took the route they had planned to take in the first place and did not just turn back because the journey was too difficult.

I am sure that in the early days of the Restrictions, people did avoid interviews with certain people because it was too much trouble and it's certainly true that potential interviewees sometimes refused to appear because their own voices would not be heard, but I believe that, overall, in the five years the Restrictions were in force the BBC here, on an almost daily basis, approached this problem with one objective in mind: that its journalism should be affected as little as possible.

In other words, if an interview with a member of Sinn Féin was relevant in a particular story before the Ban, was it any less relevant after? The answer to that, of course, was no and so we sought interviews in the normal way and figured out whether an individual's voice could be heard or not afterwards.

There have often been questions about whether the BBC did enough over the years to challenge the Ban. Should we have spent large sums of licence-payers' money pursuing the issue through the courts, both in the UK and in Europe? My own view is that we mounted the most effective challenge that there was – showing the ridiculousness of the Ban and by continuing to provide journalism which interpreted the Restriction as narrowly as possible, going about our tasks almost as if it were not there.

By way of illustration, the *Inside Story* documentary on the Maze prison is often cited as a kind of precedent-setting example because in that programme the voices of prisoners were heard speaking in a personal capacity. In other words, the views they expressed were not necessarily those of the organisations to which they belonged. It was generally thought to be the first time this interpretation had been used.

But what is often overlooked is the fact that it was a BBC Northern Ireland programme, an edition of *Spotlight* on the subject of extradition, in which voices were first used in this way and which paved the way for other programmes to come.

But however robust we were about the Ban, there was one thing that was badly affected – live broadcasting, something on which we all thrive. Thankfully, that is no longer the case.

One of the most basic attractions of broadcasting is that it allows you to see and hear people as they really are. I trust that our programmes are better with the departure of the Ban. Indeed, in that respect, you need look no further than an edition of *Spotlight* in which Mitchell McLaughlin of Sinn Féin was involved in a debate with Dr. John Dunlop, the former Presbyterian Moderator, and you will see that that might just be true.

Indeed, that was a programme which drew an extremely favourable reaction from an audience which over the years has grown increasingly more capable of handling a range of opinion, a range of views on sensitive topics, in many ways because the BBC as a broadcaster has not run away from difficult issues. Gone are the days when the switchboard was jammed after a particular interview or there was a demonstration in the front hall. Nowadays, people seem to want to be more informed and after the *Spotlight* programme I have mentioned, there were calls for more programmes like it.

I have often remarked that reporting in Northern Ireland is like reporting a General Election every day of the week. During elections, the parties and their supporters, wherever they are, either here or elsewhere in the UK, are hyper-sensitive, seeing bias at every turn, ringing up to criticise a phrase here, a headline there. As far as I am concerned, it is like that all the time. Why did you interview so-and-so and not so-and-so, why was my statement not used, why did you go to that event and not this event, why did you say that person was a Catholic but you did not say another one was a Protestant? It is a sensitive audience out there and one that keeps us on our toes.

It is therefore crucial that we get things right. It is obviously nice to get things first as well, as we did with news of the IRA ceasefire, but it is even more important to be accurate. In a community where rumour spreads like wildfire and there are a great many people around who are only too willing to fan the flames, people look to us for accuracy, for the whole story, and it is important that we provide both things, as well as a forum for discussion where none other currently exists.

That is why, over the past number of years, we have set great store in our provision of specialist correspondents in two particularly crucial areas – politics and security – and I think the work of Jim Dougal and Brian Rowan has stood out, both on the local airwaves and on network as well. And I think there is a great deal more important work to come.

But what of the violence which has dominated our headlines with a grim regularity, day after day, year after year? With Canary Wharf and the London bus explosion, have we seen the beginning of something with which we are all horribly familiar? Could there possibly be more Loughinislands, more Bloody Sundays, more days and nights with our reporters and camera crews at horrific scenes of death and destruction, more tricky judgements to be made in cutting rooms?

Believe me, the dilemmas can be many. What shots to show – how much blood – how much grief? Indeed, how much anger? The Gordon Wilsons and the Colin Parrys are very much a minority and the voice and expression of anger is as valid an emotional response in this community as that of compassion. But when does the telling of a grim story become insensitive, voyeuristic, unnecessarily distressing to the audience and ultimately self-defeating, as far as our journalism is concerned?

Like everyone else in the community, I too hoped that the violence was at an end, that we no longer had to face editorial judgements of that kind. I know that is a view shared by our staff, men and women who have spent long hours covering appalling tragedy, who have themselves made grim discoveries, such as bodies in ditches, who have been subject to threat and intimidation. These are men and women who don't just pass through. Like everyone else, they have a substantial stake in this place, and they have faced the challenges of their job with a calmness and a courage that I have never ceased to admire.

There are challenges for the future and let us hope they will be very different ones. While we all want to see a society in which violence plays no part, it will be the BBC's continuing role to report on Northern Ireland as it is, and not on a Northern Ireland created by wishful thinking.

There is more than politics and religion providing division in this society. What about unemployment, economic matters and social issues of various kinds? And what about the big universal themes of health and education? All of these things are crucial to our reporting and with the departure of violence from the agenda, for a period, there has been evidence that our journalists have been rising to the challenge and responding to the light and shade and the more diverse nature of a new environment.

But as journalists, we can't give in to a kind of collective amnesia. What happens in the future will be very much built on the experiences of the past and we will continue to report on how people are coming to terms with that, how they will cope with a changing Northern Ireland while perhaps still grieving over the death of a loved one.

The 'good news' lobby will be strong, of course, the view that we should actively promote a new Northern Ireland, and encourage the peace process. But it is not our job to be some sort of ex-officio branch of the Northern Ireland Tourist Board, to indulge in some benign form of social engineering. That would be a misuse of our responsibilities.

On the day of the IRA ceasefire, while it was hard not to feel a sense of elation inside, as if an enormous weight had been lifted, none of that came through in our reporting. Our tone that day was measured, calm, but probing, nevertheless. What were the implications of the absence of the word permanent, for example? The bigger the story, the more important it is to get the tone right.

Northern Ireland is a big story, it will continue to be one for the foreseeable future and I hope we will continue to get that tone right. It is our responsibility in the BBC to continue to probe, to investigate, to chronicle the changing times and to challenge on issues of major public importance with the vigour which I hope we have displayed thus far.

We are certainly a lot better placed to do so than we were in those distant days of 1969.

THE TROUBLE WITH REPORTING NORTHERN IRELAND

David Butler

For me, to be truthful, Media Studies is politics by another name. I am generalising of course, but I do believe that the purpose of most academic studies of the media of public communication is to investigate representation – across the range of its varying histories, styles and contents – with a view to interpreting the impact of these upon the popular mind. This is the study of symbolic power; the power of media forms to influence, shape and perhaps define, commonly-held beliefs. Does the right-wing, xenophobic and sexist character of certain of our national newspapers have the effect of producing right-wing, xenophobic and sexist outlooks among the many millions of readers who buy them daily? Or, to put it another way, maybe these particular features of the print media are no more or less than a reflection of the actual interests of their subscribers?

I have written a book called *The Trouble With Reporting Northern Ireland.*[1] It analyses the history of relationships between the British state, the broadcast media and non-fictional representation of the conflict. In the language of the trade, it could fairly be situated within the 'sociology of news' and 'cultural studies' traditions of media research in these islands. In recent months I have been reading more books about film and film theory than was possible before the completion of the manuscript. In one of these, a collection called *Shades of Noir,* Joan Copjec writes: 'the problems of film theorists are in some significant ways no different from those that beleaguer political theorists; in each case . . . analysis keeps running aground in the course of endless battles over sterile definitions'. Simply by following convention, she continues,

anyone familiar with the study of *film noir* . . . can recite a list of . . . elements thought to be necessary to the definition of the genre: a femme fatale, a morally compromised detective, an urban setting, voice-over narration, convoluted plot structure, chiaroscuro lighting, skewed framing, and so on.[2]

Now the job of a researcher and lecturer of film and cultural studies is to make meaning. Copjec is cautioning theorists and teachers of the dangers of uncritically adopting an agreed approach, for in doing so we may risk paying 'too much attention to the established terms and their relations without ever inquiring into the principle by which they are established. In virtue of what, we neglect to ask, is this particular organization instituted'.[3] What I am stressing here is that the message of any given critical judgement (the meaning made[4] by a media historian, or sociologist, semiotician, psychoanalyst etc.) depends greatly, as Copjec underlines, upon the methodological basis of the argument under construction. When addressing a contemporary film or a television documentary or news report about Northern Ireland, the manner in which the subject is conceptualised invariably constrains and directs interpretation. The answers I and others like me produce are limited by the questions we prefer to ask. There is almost always an axe to grind.

Broadcasting is believed to be important. On that much politicians, apparatchiks, broadcasters and salaried commentators readily agree. All the available evidence seems to suggest that *the* public (what in older vocabulary was often referred to, amorphously, as *the* masses or even, on occasion, as *the* people: *they,* who remain the more or less inexplicitly stated object of political interest for each of the aforesaid opinion-forming communities) thinks so too. In academic circles there is a critical consensus that the state has a definitive authority in establishing the limits of broadcasting in Britain. Among leading authors on the subject, few, if any, would dispute this basic analytical premise. Ditto, all significant recent research – variously associated with the Birmingham, Glasgow and Leicester schools of inquiry – that I can think of. Under scrutiny, however, sharp disagreements soon arise between competing uses of key terms. Some of these arguments have been explicit and detailed, conducted over an extended period. Others find expression in professional rivalries between individuals, institutions and traditions of scholarship. Reduced to a conceptual core, at issue, it seems to me, are three related questions:

(i)   Do the personnel and paraphernalia of governance in the state in Britain – civil and military bureaucracies – have a singular, coherent identity?

(ii)   Do *they* (an elite alternative to the lowly *they* referred to above) act in a unified fashion to secure their privileged interests?

(iii) Does broadcasting function as an intellectual support for the maintenance of dominant perspectives?

Looking again at the documentary studies of Cardiff and Scannell, collected as *The Social History of Broadcasting* (Blackwell, 1991), Curran and Seaton's textbook, *Power Without Responsibility* (Methuen, 1985), or any one of Briggs' authorised histories, there is a common recognition of the pivotal contribution of senior government and quasi-government mandarins – Stephen Tallents, Brendan Bracken, Noel Annan, to name just three – in the formulation of policy towards the media of public communication. At the uppermost echelon, motivations vary between departments and individuals (Foreign and Home Offices are often at odds; permanent officials routinely disagree among themselves and with ministers). At times, moreover, on specifics, there are divisions and conflicts within and between the governing institutions and affiliated interests in high society: 'the great and the good' (i.e., self-regarding public school chums who head-up quangos and semi-state bodies like the Arts Council, broadcasting authorities, the Tote) financiers, industrialists, the parasites of the royal court (in pantomime dress), old money, new money, and so on. It would be surprising indeed if the economic and political interests of these parties did not contradict one another from time to time. Though not acting in concert, and not themselves part of the ramified arrangement of governing institutions, nonetheless, this class of people, their hegemony, values and beliefs, *are* enmeshed in the priorities of the state power.[5]

I am answering 'no' and 'no' to questions (i) and (ii), but a qualified 'yes' to (iii). Returning to the rhetorical positions set out in the opening paragraph, neither caricature of the social influence of the *Sun* is satisfactory. The former is unconvincing because it relies on a 'propaganda model'[6] of state/media relations (where the categories 'elite' and 'mass' are proposed as unproblematic unities – one malign, in charge of the 'levers of power', the other passive and deceived – and where 'the mass media' is conceived, impersonally and ahistorically, as an instrument of the ruling class). Dominant interests will endeavour to dominate. This, however, cannot in itself account for the acquiescence or – perhaps less tendentiously – consent of the rest of society. To uncover and document discrimination at the level of 'sourcing' the broadcast news media, while indicative of systemic bias – and valuable for that – does not demonstrate how dominant conceptions achieve authority over the majority will. Besides other anti-democratic activities, censorship and manipulation of mass communications are conducted as a matter of routine by bureaucrats on behalf of governing organisations in the state. These, without doubt, are effective procedures. Yet popular consent for orthodox definition can surely not be attributed solely to organised lies (aka propaganda, misinformation, news management). The latter 'pluralist' explanation is not acceptable either. Reflection theories disregard the real effects of social privilege, overlooking the ways in which dominant views are casually circulated as standard; taken for granted, consistently affirmed and reaffirmed. Using the example of the Broadcasting Standards Council under the chairmanship Lord Rees-Mogg, Hood and O'Leary comment:

> regulators . . . do not make their judgements in a vacuum but on the basis of certain assumptions about the nature of society, of what is good and what is bad, about morality and the public good. In a society – like our own – which is deeply divided there is unlikely to be a consensual backing for the Council's ruling. What is one person's sense is another person's unreason. It all depends on the experience of life, on the social and class background of those who are called upon to make the judgements.[7]

Widespread social consent for the prevailing order of things is not the result of mass dupedom. There is a hierarchy of 'primary definitions' presiding over daily discourse: what John B. Thompson refers to as 'systematically asymmetrical relations of power':[8] bias, in a word, routinely mediated throughout the leading cultural institutions of civil society as common sense verities. I know no better description of this pattern of stratified authority than that offered by Stuart Hall:

Some things, people, events, relationships always get represented: always centre-stage, always in a position to define . . . to establish the terms of the conversation. Some others sometimes get represented – but always at the margin, always responding to a question whose terms and conditions have been defined elsewhere: never 'centred'. Still others are always 'represented' only by their eloquent absence . . . or refracted through the glance or gaze of others. If you are white, male, a businessman or a politician or a professional or a celebrity, your chances of getting represented will be very high. If you are black, or a woman without social status, or poor or working class or gay or powerless because you are marginal, you will always have to fight to get heard or seen. This does not mean that no one from the latter groups will ever find their way into the media. But it does mean that the structure of access to the media is systematically skewed in relation to certain social categories.[9]

Ingrained, in this way, on the institutionalised assumptions of professional broadcasting, the material effect of these ideological processes is to reinforce existing relations of domination.

Showing a regrettable preference for ultra-left evangelism over considered analysis, far too many students of the media still persist in defining listening and viewing publics as the prisoners of a species of false consciousness. (Dependent on a schematic command of theories of the state and ideology, the subtext of a great deal of work of this type is that the masses only need an infusion of the correct political prescription in order to shake off the malaise of misrecognition caused by a pernicious ruling class ideology.) Against such instrumental uses, ideology is understood here as the exercise of definitional authority: the power to 'set limits' on everyday consciousness. The institutions of broadcasting are ideologically limited by the character of their formation within the state in Britain. Study of the broadcast media therefore requires attention to the particular disposition of this decisive relationship. Within this framework of inquiry, then, the purpose of close-up reading of media texts is to study 'the way in which the specifics of works relate to structures which are not the works'.[10]

Northern Ireland has a particular and peculiar relationship to politics and society in Britain, as *British* broadcasting *in* Northern Ireland does to centrally-determined norms. The development of local broadcasting may be seen as an analogue of the troubled relations between these islands. Public Service Broadcasting was the product of an extended period of minority government in Britain (1910-45). The formation of the state in Northern Ireland was likewise shaped by the coalitionist character of Westminster politics and by the trend towards corporatism in the economy and industrial relations during the interwar years. The bipartisan nature of political broadcasting in the 1950s and 1960s was a fair reflection of a comfy concordat between the leaderships of the two government parties on the fundamentals of the post-war settlement. Like the NHS and other leading institutions of the welfare state, the assault on the *independence* of broadcasting by the Thatcher governments (1979-90) was symptomatic of the regime's spiteful opposition to the structures of the social democratic consensus (minimally understood as policies for demand-led growth, full employment and universal provision of public education, housing, health insurance etc.). Organically bound to the conditions of its liberal democratic formation, public service broadcasting is an ideologically limiting system; limited, that is to say, to the prevailing nostrums of the Age of Consent. For while consensus broadcasting assures *impartiality* as between major parties in the political nation, balanced coverage also confines representation to a narrow purview of *responsible* interests. Historically, broadcasting in Britain favours the 'middle ground' of politics and society. By the same token, *irresponsible* viewpoints – those voices deemed as threatening to the status quo – have tended to be marginalised by the centripetal inclinations of the consensus mode of regulation. (In mid-1960s Britain, the governing classes regarded Enoch Powell, an early advocate of neo-liberalism allied to aggressive English nationalism, and his brand of proto-Thatcherism as beyond the pale.)[11]

The projection of an integrative, centralising vision of 'national unity' has been endemic to the constitution of broadcasting since its inception in the state in the 1920s. Indeed, arguably, sustaining the appearance of a culture of 'oneness' has been the ideological invariable that defines the historic mission of broadcasting in Britain. Always more imaginary than real, for a time (until the collapse of the 'long boom' years of relative international prosperity) the false homogeneity of this institutionalised accommodation was, at the least, a politically tenable means of regulating economy and society. Whatever its merits in relation to post-war Britain (England, Scotland and Wales), the typical consensus model of civil organisation was manifestly untenable in the fissiparous conditions of Northern Ireland. The limits of the unitary state in Britain are fairly secure. Scottish and Welsh separatists are of fractional significance; left/right disputation is carried on within settled constitutional boundaries. Even after the disruptions of the Thatcher era, the legitimacy (definitional authority) of key *national* institutions is not at issue (and will certainly stand Blairite reform without serious risk to the stability of the ruling order).

'Twoness', rather than 'oneness' defines political and cultural life in Northern Ireland. Ours is a conflicted, dissensual society. At base, the years of killing were a consequence of conceptual disagreement: the conflict (continued by belligerent and/or passive methods) is about and between opposing meanings of the limits of the political nation. Consequently, we have endless disputes over terms of reference. The absence of definitional authority, of agreed or neutral codes, results in a profound crisis of representation. This is the trouble with reporting Northern Ireland. Prefigured on unitary principles – upon the organisation of consent – public service broadcasting has the gravest difficulty satisfying a fundamentally divided polity. Founded on centrist diagnosis, network coverage, by and large, sees the conflict along moderate/extreme faultlines where, in fact, no such simple cleavage pertains. Particularism is at the root of the conflict in Northern Ireland. Disturbances arise because nationalist and republican aims delegitimise unionist and loyalist claims, and vice versa. There can be no impartial outcome where the advance of one perspective may only be achieved at the expense of the other. A moderate solution, in this dissensual context, will depend on the defeated party (or parties) settling for less than the absolute, in order to restrict their losses. Differences of emphasis within republican and loyalist blocs do exist, but these are not reducible to the hard-line/moderate, hawks/doves shorthand preferred by too many journalists.

In place of the taxonomy of 'extremism' (where 'terrorism' was treated as irrational, apolitical gangsterism), from the late-70s, local broadcasting has increasingly sought to represent the parties of physical force in terms of their 'relevance' to local developments. Indirectly and grudgingly, this policy shift (formalised by BBC NI in 1977) had the effect of recognising the political rationale and popularity of paramilitarism; instead, that is, of denying them access on the basis of monstrous illegitimacy, as was the habit of network coverage. For the first time, furthermore, the author of the statement on 'broadcasting to a community in conflict', the late Richard Francis,[12] explicitly admitted the inappropriateness of seeking to manufacture consensus where none existed. Acknowledging the reality of a dissensus society, in the period since – censorship and intimidation notwithstanding – local broadcasting achieved a more adequate description of the basis of the conflict than was permissible under the terms of the terrorism-as-cause paradigm dominating national coverage. Through the 1980s, in circumstances when, for fear of compromise, unionist politicians could not agree to be in the same place at the same time as their nationalist counterparts, and in the absence of a representative political forum, both BBC NI and UTV have performed a critically mediative role, facilitating dialogue that could not otherwise occur (where dialogue is understood, minimally, as the juxtaposing of separately recorded testimonies into a continuous sequence, thus effecting the impression of conversation).

The point in all of this is to demonstrate how the dislocation of regional from UK wide forms suggests that understanding the peculiarities of British broadcasting in Northern Ireland requires particular, detailed knowledge(s) of the local context. To read off meaning by applying a general theory is to risk misinterpretation.

My aim in this short essay has been to sketch the theoretical outline of a non-reductive approach to the study of British broadcasting and Northern Ireland, stressing the close relationship between research methodologies and the message delivered up by academic analysis. *Interpreting Northern Ireland* (the title of John Whyte's indispensable textbook: Clarendon Press, 1991) is a doubly difficult business. First, due to the double-codedness of local political cultures, every utterance has a dual interpretation attached and, quite often, a dual intent. This is perfectly apparent in the ongoing 'peace process' (meaning the constitutionalising of Sinn Féin), as Gerry Adams' recent faux pas on the matter of the IRA not having 'gone away' afterall ably illustrated. And second, the reader is advised that critically informed commentaries on Northern Ireland are not generally innocent or neutrally coded. Writing here as a critic of broadcasting, who, like a film historian or 'a historian of art or politics, proposes an explanatory argument. Having asked a "How?" or "Why?" question, he puts forward an answer, based on an examination of evidence in the light of assumptions and background knowledge',[11] I am bound to say, in conclusion, the explanations arrived at in critical works almost inevitably reveal political sympathies (or at any rate will be represented as having done so).

NOTES

1. David Butler, *The Trouble With Reporting Northern Ireland* (Aldershot: Avebury, 1995).
2. Joan Copjec (ed.), *Shades of Noir: A Reader* (London: Verso, 1993), p. xi.
3. ibid.
4. A reference to David Bordwell, *Making Meaning: Inference and Rhetoric in the Interpretation of Cinema* (Harvard: Harvard University Press, 1989).
5. On the anatomy of the state in contemporary Britain, see Will Hutton, *The State We're In* (London: Jonathan Cape, 1995). On competing theories of the state see, David Held, 'Central Perspectives on the modern state', in Held et al, *States and Societies* (Oxford: Blackwell/Oxford University Press, 1983); also John Keane, *The Media and Democracy* (Oxford: Polity, 1991).
6. 'The mass media serve as a system for communicating messages and symbols to the general populace. It is their function to amuse, entertain, and inform, and to inculcate individuals with the values, beliefs, and codes of behaviour that will integrate them into the institutional structures of the larger society. In a world of concentrated wealth and major conflicts of class interest, to fulfil this role requires systematic propaganda.' Edward S. Herman & Noam Chomsky, *Manufacturing Consent: the Political Economy of the Mass Media* (New York: Pantheon Books, 1988), p.1.
7. Stuart Hood & Garret O'Leary, *Questions of Broadcasting* (London: Methuen, 1990), p.189.
8. John B. Thompson, *Ideology and Modern Culture: Critical Social Theory in the Era of Mass Communication* (Oxford: Polity, 1990), p.7.
9. Stuart Hall, 'Media Power and Class Power', in James Curran, Jake Ecclestone, Giles Oakley & Alan Richardson (eds.), *Bending Reality* (London: Pluto, 1986), p.9.
10. Raymond Williams (in conversation with Edward Said), 'Media, Margins and Modernity', in Raymond Williams, *The Politics of Modernism: Against the New Conformists* (London: Verso, 1989), p.185.
11. See Andrew Gamble, *The Free Economy and the Strong State: the Politics of Thatcherism* (Houndmills: Macmillan, 1988).
12. Richard Francis, 'Broadcasting to a Community in Conflict – the Experience of Northern Ireland', lecture to Royal Institute of International Affairs, Chatham House, London (22 February, 1977). Following Francis's formulation, see also Tom Kelly, *Politics, Terrorism and the Media: a Reporter's role in a Polarised Society* (Cambridge: BP Fellowship Paper, 1986).
13. Kristin Thompson, David Bordwell, *Film History: An Introduction* (New York: McGraw-Hill, 1994) p. xxxv.

THE LONG HAUL TO EQUALITY:
WOMEN JOURNALISTS AT THE BBC IN BELFAST

Liz Fawcett

'When I first came here I . . . felt very much the outsider and very igno-rant. I went to pub with three male colleagues. One of them had been sent porno photos through the internal post from someone – [one of the men] took them out and went on and on and pointed to bits of anatomy and said "That must be you Barbara". But there was a bullying side to it. The other two men were also being quite abusive. In the end I was close to tears and I thought "You bastards. I'm not going to let you see me cry". So I said "I'm just going shopping, I'll see you back at the office". So I disappeared and tried to get myself together. Afterwards, [one of the men] said "I'm sorry if we upset you in any way but it's just the craic". He was trying to excuse sex-ist attitudes as Irish culture.'

'When I joined the BBC . . . as a freelance, within a few months I got an attachment and while I was on attachment, I was pregnant. I never missed a single day due to my pregnancy. I was a good employee. There were men who went out drinking during working hours who rang in sick with hang-overs. It doesn't happen so much now but it did then . . . Their behaviour seemed to be just accepted at the time. . . . I left to have my son and came back . . . and then a job came up and I went for it and got it. My manager then had a policy of letting people who showed promise go over from the radio-desk to television . . . This didn't happen to me . . . So I brought this to the attention of the then radio news editor who said "Well, you were hav-ing babies and things."'

Those unhappy stories would have surprised few women who worked in the BBC's Belfast newsroom seven or eight years ago. It was a 'macho' environment dominated, at an informal level, by a drinking culture which largely excluded women. More impor-tantly, all sorts of unquestioned assumptions went unchallenged; if you were a woman and wanted to have babies, that was your problem; if you got a hard time from the camera crews and couldn't take it, tough; if you thought you were getting too many 'soft' stories . . . well, women are good at doing those heart-rending interviews, aren't they. . .?

When I joined BBC Northern Ireland as a budding reporter in 1987, I have to say I probably shared all those assumptions myself. It is not that I, and indeed many other people, would have actually voiced such attitudes in such a bald way. It is just that I rarely demurred if I was given the 'soft' story. I assumed any decision to have children would inevitably have an adverse effect on my career and would be entirely my problem. Furthermore, I took difficulties with crews for granted and scarcely mentioned them to colleagues. Indeed, I only realised how much needless stress such behaviour was causing me when I went to London and discovered what it was like to be taken seriously by all – as opposed to just some – of my colleagues on the technical side. Why was I so naive? Quite simply because journalism is portrayed as a tough profession that requires tough people. It never occurred to me that, while journalism is undoubtedly a challenging career, it did not necessarily have to be quite as unpleasant and pressurised as I assumed!

During the eight years I spent with the BBC, the 'macho' culture slowly began to fade; several of the chief stalwarts of the 'drinking' fraternity left, as did some older technical staff. At the same time, changes were afoot in the Personnel department. The BBC nationally had embarked on a concerted effort to improve the representation of women among its staff, and to ensure women really did have equality of opportunity. At Broadcasting House in Belfast, radical plans were drawn up to drag recalcitrant male managers into the new non-sexist and equality-led BBC. In 1992, the then Head of Personnel, Ruth Laird, came up with a highly ambitious 'Agenda for Positive Action', or so it seemed at the time. Managers were to attend workshops for training on 'gender awareness' and 'anti-discrimination', phrases guaranteed to get many male journalists shaking their heads in disbelief. When I read the proposals not long after they had been drafted, I could not see such plans being implemented without either outright opposition or, at least, distinct lack of enthusiasm on the part of many male managers.

A 'Family Friendly' BBC

Yet, three years on (at the time of writing), Ms. Laird's 'Agenda' seems to be making a considerable impact in News and Current

Affairs. Female staff, who would have been deeply cynical about any 'equal opportunities' promises by either Personnel or management are suddenly full of praise, or at least far less critical than was once the case. One 'watershed' has been the decision to grant one woman journalist a job-share, and another permission to work part-time. In both cases, the women concerned wanted to be able to spend more time with their children. As far as anyone can remember, these are the first instances of female journalists at the BBC in Belfast being shown such flexibility by the organisation.

The news has been welcomed by women but has caused some raised eyebrows among the men. One female journalist described their reaction:

> Somebody will point their finger and say 'Oh look, she's getting . . .' The problem is the 'bandinos' among the boys, where their wives make all the arrangements. They don't realise what it's like.

In fact, these options are also available to men who, I was assured, will be treated on exactly the same basis as any women who apply. The woman quoted above was also worried that, by opting for a special arrangement, such as a job-share, 'you might be cutting off your nose to spite your face'; in other words, she was concerned it would only count against someone if they subsequently went for a promotion. Anna Carragher, BBC Northern Ireland's Head of Programmes, is adamant that that should not be the case. Ms. Carragher has three children herself; while working for the BBC in London, she requested – and got – a transfer from a programme with extremely long and unpredictable hours to one that enabled her to spend more time with her children. She does not feel this move impeded her career progression at all. However, prior to that, she spent several years combining overnight shifts on programmes such as BBC Radio's Today with bringing up her own children while they were still very young. She does feel you cannot expect to work 'office hours' in broadcast journalism:

> Of course I'd hope any management would be very sympathetic and take into account the problems that anybody, man or woman, has . . . but broadcasting is an occupation which demands irregular working.

While BBC Northern Ireland is making great strides in terms of what it calls its 'family friendly' policies in many respects, there has been one setback; in December, 1994, it closed a crèche which it had been running for about eighteen months because it was judged to be too great a drain on finances. However, Ms. Carragher maintains such a facility is of limited use to journalistic staff:

> It's one of those principled things that people are in favour of, but not necessarily for them themselves personally. . .and I think that's particularly the case for women and men who are working in news and current affairs – the more senior, the more journalistic areas – because they're the people, the very nature of their job – it does involve irregular-hour working. . . . Therefore they will tend to need much more round the clock child-care and most people don't want to tuck their baby up in a crèche at eight o'clock at night. They want their baby in its own cot at eight o'clock at night. Therefore, in a sense, they want more individual child-care, tailored to their individual needs. And I think culturally Belfast is . . . it's very difficult to get that kind of child-care.

Anna Carragher has personal experience of this type of problem; shortly before I interviewed her, she had just advertised for someone to come in during the afternoons to look after her two school-age children. Despite the fact she was prepared to pay a reasonable wage and the work was hardly arduous, Ms. Carragher had not had one single reply. She was quite sure that, in London, she would have been inundated with responses.

A New Climate

Where once female staff were extremely reluctant to raise child-care problems with their managers for fear their commitment to the job would be questioned, now managers are required to encourage staff to discuss such concerns. The main means of doing this is an employee's annual performance appraisal interview. Performance appraisal was only introduced recently in the BBC, in the face of much hostility from staff. Not all the women I spoke to were impressed with the system, but some certainly welcomed it and felt their worries were being taken seriously.

It is not just journalists who undergo performance appraisal, however. Managers are also subject to the same yearly review, and part of their appraisal examines their ability to effectively implement equal opportunities policies. When asked for a concrete example of the impact this had had in News and Current Affairs, Anna Carragher said moves were being made to reduce the amount of bad language used in the newsroom. This information was greeted with wry smiles by former colleagues who felt it was hardly the most pressing problem, although it clearly offended someone as informal complaints had been made.

However, it does seem that a more fundamental change is occurring; a new working culture seems to be developing in which staff at all levels are realising they can be held accountable for the way they behave. At the time of writing, journalists were still talking about one internal case which has not been made public and in which the particular complaints were not upheld. Nevertheless, one female journalist said it had made a big difference to the way women were treated:

> It's made a lot of the ANEs [Assistant News Editors] – who are mostly men – very aware of how to treat women and of what type of stories to give them. Mind you, there are jibes. . . 'If you do such and such to [two of the women who made complaints], you know what'll happen'. . . . But they're not meant in a sinister way. . . . It's made people a lot more aware about what you can do if you're not happy with the way you're being treated.[1]

Indeed, this particular journalist says she was belittled by a cameraman in front of a room full of men. 'But I spoke to him afterwards and there has been a complete change'. One has to be careful not to tar all technical staff with the same brush; most are a pleasure to work with. Relatively few individuals are perceived as making reporter's lives unnecessarily stressful through constant carping. Furthermore, it remains unclear whether female reporters suffer more than their male colleagues in this respect. The above journalist is quite adamant women do come off worse. However, Anna Carragher says one must be wary about assuming women are more vulnerable in the face of this type of bullying behaviour:

> I think some women are extremely vulnerable and some men are extremely vulnerable. I mean I do think it's an individual

thing. I don't like the idea, I mean I really don't like the idea that you say 'Women react like this' and not take women as individuals. Some women can be tough as old boots and some men can crumble easily and vice versa. And I actually think it's quite offensive to say 'Women are like this'

There is no doubt, however, that women are becoming much more prepared to stand up for themselves. One result of this appears to have been a reduction in sexist comments, at least those made in the company of women who find them offensive. As one female producer observed:

I think most of the women, even at RJ [Regional Journalist] level, are more prepared to say 'Look, can we change this conversation?' or just to walk away.

Indeed, she believes News and Current Affairs is now witnessing the emergence of a small but growing breed of truly non-sexist men who would be just as likely as the women to object to prejudiced comments.

Newsrooms: A Reflection of Society?

When I interviewed Anna Carragher she had only recently moved to her new job from London. I asked her how BBC Northern Ireland compared to the BBC in London in terms of attitudes towards women and their representation in the organisation:

There are more women at a more senior level in London. Again, it's not perfect. But it is more commonplace, without doubt, to find women at a fairly senior level and I think that does make a difference. I mean I don't actually see such a huge difference in the attitude of the BBC. The BBC has got an equal opportunities policy – a 'Managing Diversity' policy – which actually permeates the entire corporation. The selection procedures we have here, the fair selection training that I've done in Northern Ireland – I also did fair selection training in England. . . I think what is different is the attitude of the society as well. I think this is still a much, much more macho society than – well, I'm not saying that London society is not macho – but it certainly pays lip-service a great deal more than the society here does.

Perhaps the past 26 years play a part in that. The conflict has dominated life in Northern Ireland, and dominated the news agenda. While female journalists at BBC Northern Ireland frequently covered political and security stories, the journalists who made up the specialist teams in these areas were all men at the time of writing. Thus, a woman may provide viewers or listeners with the facts about a particular incident. However, if an editor feels greater explanation is needed, it will always be a man who adds gravitas by giving an in-depth analysis. Anna Carragher suggested the monopoly of male experts in this area was probably at least partly a result of the fact the key players in these fields tend to be men. 'There are not many women politicians', she reminded me.

Our television screens are certainly evidence of that; most of the interviewees in both political and security-related stories have tended to be men. Whether they are politicians or policemen, male interviewees are the voices of authority in such stories; when women appear, they are the humble folk whose relative has just been killed, who happened to witness an incident or who happened to get picked for a 'vox pop' interview, aimed at sounding out 'grassroots' opinion.

Traditionally, of course, stories involving violence and/or politics have been found at the top of news bulletins. In this sense, the ceasefires (which were still holding at the time of writing) should be good news for women, allowing them a greater and a more 'authoritative' voice. The general feeling among the female journalists I spoke to seemed to be that stories concerning health, education and the environment were being given greater prominence. Indeed, even before the ceasefires, audience research was clearly indicating there was an appetite for these type of issues among viewers of Inside Ulster which was not being met. Their opinions were being taken very seriously at the time of writing; in terms of viewing figures, BBC NI's early evening TV news magazine, *Inside Ulster*, was outmatched by its UTV rival. Although management is anxious to stress publicly that BBC NI is not obsessed with ratings, my conversations with journalists suggested there was a drive to improve them and, therefore, provide more coverage of the sort of stories viewers wanted. It would seem audience demand had combined with the ceasefires to produce a quite considerable shift in 'news values', although one senior journalist I spoke to insisted the change had not been radical enough, thus far.

Equal Ambition?

As Table 1 shows the position of women in News and Current Affairs in Belfast has improved quite considerably over a relatively short period, in terms of the posts they hold. As can be seen, however, women were still poorly represented in the most senior grades when these figures were compiled. At the time of writing, a major overhaul of the management structure in News and Current Affairs meant a number of managerial-level posts had just been created, giving women an unrivalled opportunity to move up the ladder into positions of real influence. One woman had been asked by her own manager if she would be interested in going into management. She intended to apply for one of the less 'prestigious' posts but was well aware that she was an eminently suitable candidate for one of the more sought-after and more demanding jobs. Yet, now that such a prize was within her grasp, she was prevaricating:

> I don't play the political game well. . . . .And [one senior female manager] seems to be there from early morning to night. I don't fancy that. . . . And I don't want to be on call twenty-four hours a day at the moment. . . . I don't know. I'll wait and see.

Her children were her main concern, which perhaps brings us back to the point Anna Carragher made about the 'macho' culture in Northern Ireland, and the way it permeates into the home and into the career choices of women. However, it is not simply a question of a 'macho' culture forcing women to choose between careers and kids. The above comments also highlight some of the less enviable and more stressful aspects of most jobs in top management; many men and women – with or without children – would not necessarily relish the long hours and 'internal politics' that tend to accompany such jobs.

However, the woman quoted above was doubtless also weighing up the possible consequences of *not* applying for a top job when she was seen as a prime candidate. Another female journalist, speaking to me about the same vacancies in casual conversation, told me she intended to go for one of the posts, adding, by way of explanation, 'I really think I ought to be seen to be going for it'. Maybe she felt a need to cover up the real degree of ambition that lay within her; on the other hand, perhaps she was acknowledging she was not being entirely true to herself and her own needs in applying for the job.

One only needs to read Ginny Dougary's *The Executive Tart and Other Myths* [2] to be put off senior media management for life. One top editor is quoted as saying:

> I am prepared to do anything to get what I want. . ..I know how to get around men . . . by being charming, by letting them think that they're cleverer than me, by being mildly flirtatious . . . Everything is an act, a game. Everything is a means to an end. [3]

A leading media buyer tells Dougary she did not leave work to see her husband when he was in intensive care with a brain tumour:

> Why should I? Maybe I'm selfish, but we've always led separate lives. His illness has hardened me, if anything. But when the time comes, I hope my senior colleagues will give me leave of absence. [4]

There is no doubt that managers at BBC Northern Ireland would be aghast at the idea that one had to become as 'hard' and out of touch with 'human' values as these two women seemed to have. Nevertheless, if women are equivocating as they get one foot in the board room, it should perhaps lead us to ask whether, in fact, the nature of the management job itself needs to change. Dr. Judi Marshall, referring to health professionals, observes:

> When people devote much of their energy to impressing others and to image-management, they are likely to restrict effectiveness. They look to superiors for affirmation rather than giving relationships with clients primacy. Much of the career planning literature for women tells them to accept these as 'realities'. I do not think them inevitable. Many women do not want to be identified with this cynical view of organisations. They want to take task quality (in which relationships and people are typically key ingredients) as their prime criterion of achievement, and do not want to become involved in image-management and organisational politics. [5]

It has to be said, however, that Anna Carragher confounds any stereotype of a 'tough as nails' female manager. She is pleasant, genuine, does not 'power dress' and lacks both that cold female version of 'machismo' and the 'matronly' manner that seem to constitute the two stereotypes of women who have reached the top; stereotypes which sadly many women do seem to feel they have to live up to when they reach such positions.

Having said this, Ms. Carragher has already shown her determination to implement change where she feels change is needed and she undoubtedly works long hours. Nevertheless, those female journalists I spoke to seemed impressed by her sincerity and by her reputation for treating staff as equals rather than inferiors. Perhaps, then, she will act as a role model for women who would like to try management but don't want to have to take on an unpleasant or alien personality in the process. It would be nice to return to Broadcasting House in the not-too-distant future and find at least a few women at the helm in News and Current Affairs. Hopefully, News and Current Affairs will remain the more 'female friendly' department it seems to have become. My one concern is the fact that fear of retribution is one of the main factors which has prompted change. I am quite sure that, if women did fill some of the most senior positions, there would be less concern about acting in a 'politically correct' way for fear of disciplinary or legal action, and more concern about simply giving everyone an equal opportunity to develop their potential.

Liz Fawcett worked as a journalist with BBC Northern Ireland from 1987-1994, latterly as Education Correspondent. Some of the above interview material is taken from interviews conducted with a number of former colleagues in 1994. The interview with Anna Carragher, and further brief interviews with female journalists, were carried out in August, 1995. The name used in the quote at the beginning of the chapter is a pseudonym. The author would like to thank Anna Carragher and BBC Northern Ireland for their help in providing information for this chapter.

Table 1: Journalists' posts in BBC Northern Ireland's News and Current Affairs Department in Belfast (March 1994/August 1995).

	Male		Female	
	1994	1995	1994	1995
Head, News and Current Affairs	1	1	–	–
Editors	4	4	–	–
Chief Producer, Radio Current Affairs	1	1	–	–
Senior Producer, Radio Current Affairs	1	1	–	–
Assistant News Editors	5	4	–	–
Correspondents	4	5	1	1
Producers, TV Current Affairs	2	1	–	1
Reporters	11	11	4	7
Producers, Radio Current Affairs	3	4	2	2
Senior Production Journalist	–	–	1	1
Production Journalists	–	–	–	3
Assistant Producer, TV Current Affairs	–	–	1	–
Regional Journalists	8	6	5	6
Regional News Trainee	1	–	–	1
TOTAL	41	38	14	22

Women as percentage of total journalists in News and Current Affairs:

25.45% in March 1994
36.67% in August 1995

A number of job titles are categorised at about the same grade. The ordering in the above table is not a 'strict' hierarchy. However, the more senior jobs are at the top of the table, while the more junior jobs are at the bottom. For the sake of simplicity, some job titles have been amalgamated into one category. The table does not include freelances.

NOTES

1. In fact all the Assistant News Editors were men at the time of writing (see Table 1). Other staff would have 'acted up' as ANEs, from time to time, however.
2. Ginny Dougary, *The Executive Tart and Other Myths: Media Women Talk Back* (London: Virago Press,1994).
3. Sue Douglas, Executive Editor, Sunday Times quoted in Dougary, *The Executive Tart*, p.136.
4. Christine Walker, leading media buyer with the media agency, Zenith quoted in Dougary, p.229.
5. Judi Marshall, *Thinking about Women and Careers*, working paper for Opportunity 2000: Managing Gender and Improving Service Effectiveness, NHS Research Workshop1992, (unpublished), p.2.

THE BBC GOVERNORS:
PAST, PRESENT AND FUTURE*

Ken Bloomfield

I suppose the title I have chosen – 'the BBC Governors: past, present and future' – has a faintly Dickensian ring to it; and I will indeed be bringing a few ghosts to many people's bedside in the course of this article. Indeed, I often think of Dickens when debate rages – as it sometimes does – around the concept of 'high quality programmes'; that giant of the nineteenth century novel who introduced many of his works to the public by instalments in what might be described as the 'soaps' of the written word.

In venturing into this territory of governance I speak with the very modest experience of somewhat less than five years as the Northern Ireland National Governor of the BBC. I have, on the other hand, been much concerned in a previous career with shaping various organs of Government and seeking to identify structures and people capable of running them.

The title 'Governor' does not of itself pin down with any great precision the nature of the powers or influence to be enjoyed by its holder. One has to look no further than the history of the Commonwealth to appreciate that at different times, and in different places, the Governor of a territory may find a place at almost any point along a spectrum from near-absolute to wholly constitutional monarch. It is a theme on which I would enjoy listening to Chris Patten at some future time.

In the case of the BBC I would identify at least four sets of influences which have determined the question of how its Governors have acted, or do act, at any particular point in its history. There is, first, what I might call the 'statutory framework', although at the centre of it there has been for many years not an Act of Parliament but a Royal Charter. Second, there is what I might call the 'case law' of the BBC; the steady accretion of custom and practice in its governance, building up over time to rather well-established conventions. Third, there is the influence of the working environment current at a particular time. It is inevitably the case that management of an institution in crisis, under scrutiny or in a state of radical change presents quite different challenges from management in a steady state. And finally there is the influence of powerful personalities. All of us who have worked in large, complex organisations know that the realities of power and influence are not always obvious on the face of organisation charts.

Before I attempt to set out where the Governors fit into the scheme of the contemporary BBC and what role they might most usefully play in the future, I would like to remind you all of how these sets of influences, as I have described them, have shaped the role and function of the Governors to date.

So let us begin with the formal framework. Since January 1927, under successive Royal Charters, the properties and powers of the British Broadcasting Corporation have been vested in its Board of Governors, who constitute the body corporate. Lord Crawford's committee of 1925 had recognised the need for a highly responsible body with an independent status to develop broadcasting in the national interest along the lines which had already been established by the British Broadcasting Company. Since then we have had the Second Charter of 1937, the Third Charter of 1947, the Fourth Charter of 1952, the Fifth Charter of 1964, and Supplemental Charters of 1969, 1974, 1976 and 1979 leading up to the present Charter granted in 1981 which expires on 31 December 1996. Over that period the successive Charters have clarified the position of what was then the Empire Service and authorised a World Service, taken account of the development of television alongside the original radio broadcasting, and caught up with many other matters of detail, but have not materially changed or substantially defined the constitutional role of Governors as envisaged and established by the First Charter.

Frankly, none of the Charters has set out the specific role expected of Governors, as distinct from management. The Governors are the Corporation. In that sense, it is correct to say that the Governors are the BBC – neither more nor less than the corporate body identified in the Charter. The key provisions of the present Charter which touch on the role of Governors are Articles 1 and 12

(1) Incorporation: The Corporation shall continue to be a body corporate by the name of the British Broadcasting Corporation. . . . The Governors of the Corporation shall be the members thereof . . .

(12) Organisation: The Corporation shall appoint such officers and staff as it may from time to time consider necessary for the efficient performance of its function and transaction of its business. . . .

In practice, it has always been accepted that there are limits to the Governors' role. In the earliest years of the BBC's existence, Reith and the then Governors disagreed from time to time about where those limits should be set. However, in 1931 – as it happens, the year of my birth – Reith and the then BBC Chairman John Whitley agreed a definition of the Governors' role in a memorandum including the key statement that: 'The Governors of the BBC act primarily as trustees to safeguard the broadcasting service in the national interest. Their functions are not executive . . .' The Whitley Memorandum was to be questioned by the Beveridge Committee, reporting in 1951, and the Government White Paper of 1952 which took the line that the position of the Governors should be defined only by the Charter. This, however, was really begging the question. The powers conferred by the Charter were wide, general and absolute; there would be disorder and misunderstanding in the absence of any generally accepted convention about their exercise. On the whole the Governors continued to operate within the spirit of the Whitley Memorandum, which was subsequently updated and expanded in a 'letter to a new Governor' written by a Board member, Sir John Johnston in 1982, approved by his colleagues, and subsequently made available to new Governors on appointment. It included certain key phrases worth recalling today:-

'the general government of the BBC must be by retrospective review. . .

'they (the Governors) have made a single huge act of delegation, by which they have entrusted the Director General and his staff with the implementation of the purposes for which the Corporation was established'

'the Board is apprehended by those working in the Corporation as the conscience of the BBC, and the ultimate guardian of its public service ethos'

'the means at their disposal are primarily their power to appoint the senior staff; their power to authorise expenditure; and what one might term their general power to call to account'.

'we are not editors, though we are not indifferent to the editorial function. Indeed we may, on behalf of the public, have to sit in judgement on editorial decisions. We must therefore be detached from them, not a part of them'

'equally, we are not managers . . . Our concern must be with performance, and with the general efficiency of the management function we have delegated'

The Whitley Memorandum and the Johnston Letter were, if you like, important codifications of the custom and practice and the working conventions of the BBC.

So has it always worked like that in practice? Not exactly, Lord Copper! For we are dealing with a human institution, whose affairs have been conducted from time to time by powerful personalities. Any study of the relationships between Chairmen and Directors General would illustrate a range of models of human behaviour. In particular, where lines of demarcation are not relatively clear and specific, the more powerful personality of the time will in practice occupy any disputed ground.

Let me turn now to my personal experience. I must confess that joining the Board of Governors in August 1991 could best be compared with being called off the sub's bench at Twickenham or Lansdowne Road deep into a fast and furious, highly-competitive match. Because my native Northern Ireland is a small place and I had known personally almost all of my predecessors as National Governor, I did not labour under any illusion that I was accepting some cushy billet for my retirement. My immediate predecessor, after all, had entered the Board Room with the din of the *Real Lives* controversy ringing in his ears. Even so, I was ill-prepared for the extraordinary degree of media interest in our recent doings. It took a little time to get used to the experience of finding, at a weekend, apparently authoritative accounts of one's presumed, assumed or imagined position on some controversial issue, not infrequently mutually contradicting each other. It was revealing, too, to be assailed both by people who assumed we were 'interfering' in every aspect of day to day work, including the editorial and programme-making responsibilities of BBC management, and by others who called on us to 'get a grip' on the organisation, usually in some wholly undefined, or at best extremely ill-defined way.

My own experience indicated from the outset that there was a great deal to be done without usurping the legitimate roles of the Director General and the Corporation's management. I believe it to be necessary for a Governor to be visible, both inside and outside the BBC; to visit BBC staff and BBC events around the country; to encounter the public at open meetings and by other means; to listen to what is being said to us through the GAC and other elements of a complex advisory machinery.

I found at least three aspects of our business gave me some cause for concern. The organisation generated a great deal of paper. Governors received media extracts by the sack full, and a huge amount of reading matter and data for information. It is a dilemma familiar to any Minister in government. He must have a right to see everything which may be relevant; but can he actually read it all and find time to run the Department? Here a good Private Office would be a great help in terms of filtering out, summarising, or separating the real matters deserving attention from those needing no more than a quick scan. Governors of the BBC do not have Private Offices, although National Governors are more fortunate than other colleagues – with the exception of the Chairman and Vice-Chairman – in at least having offices to sit in and local staff with some ability to support them. I do not suggest for one moment that we support Governors with their own private bureaucracy; but rather that we need to be insistent on good discipline in the nature of information submitted to us.

Second, I identified at an early stage the old problem of the tyranny of the Agenda. Meeting even twice a month, we would have at each meeting a hefty agenda of business. Many of the issues under discussion, at this time of Charter Renewal, were of great complexity and importance. Sometimes one had to abandon useful lines of discussion to allow the whole agenda to move forward. I believe it has been a very good move to adopt, as we have now done, a pattern of monthly formal meetings with a more rigorously disciplined agenda, interleaved with less formal meetings of the Governors without an agenda, allowing weighty issues of current importance to be discussed without constraining time limits, often in face to face dialogue with the member of the Board of Management most directly responsible.

And then there is the crucial question of our role in relation to programmes. Fascinating though discussions about structure, finance and staffing may be, all this elaborate infrastructure is for the purpose of making excellent programmes. It is by programmatic standards – not alone but to a very large extent – that the BBC must be and will be judged. When I joined the Board of Governors it was a well-established practice to devote part of the time at each Board meeting to the comments of Governors on programmes. Occasionally we would discuss programmes in prospect, often in the context of a wider presentation by a channel controller or other senior manager of part of the output. We would never, in my experience, discuss programme detail, scrutinise a script or preview a programme. Our comments were overwhelmingly post facto. I confess that, initially, I found our role in this respect frustrating and ill-defined. It would seem as absurd to detach Governors from the question of programmes and programme quality as to allow non-executive directors of a soap company to discuss anything except soap. There is, though, a dilemma here familiar to anyone who has examined the lay influence on professional mysteries. We commonly see, for example, in Police Authorities, an inherent tension between an Authority's wish to represent the public interest and a Chief Constable's attachment to his operational autonomy. It has been rare to have on the Board of Governors of the BBC anyone with substantial previous experience of programme-making, and I suspect it is not easy to make the transition from one role to the other. I doubt if his period as a member of the Board was Hugh Greene's most happy or successful period at the BBC. As it is, we are twelve individuals with our respective tastes, interests and prejudices which will not necessarily conform to those of the national audience (which, of course, begs the very large question of whether there is such a thing!). I often recall a television interview years ago with the late Cecil King, when the interviewer asked him, in effect, how a man of his cultivated nature could enjoy the *Daily Mirror* and King replied, 'But I don't produce the *Daily Mirror* for people like me'. And it is, incidentally, generally unwise to assume that a taste different from one's own is necessarily a lower taste, as if there were a table of tastes as fixed as the table of elements.

None of this is to suggest that the Governors should have no role at all in relation to programmes as trustees of the public interest. They need to understand the principal considerations underlying a particular genre of the output, and this is best done by including in the schedule of Board meetings provision for methodical consideration through the year of each substantial segment, not to reach immediate decisions but to inform Governors as they come to consider the adoption, rolling forward or modification of a coherent programme strategy. The aim must be to enable Governors not just to say 'I liked this' or 'I didn't like that', but rather to consider whether the programmes transmitted, individually and taken together, have been consistent with a strategic approach to broadcasting which has at its heart and core the public interest.

Does this mean that Governors should be reluctant to comment post facto on individual programmes, and should in no circumstances ever again seek to view or hear an individual programme before transmission? I would not myself carry the argument so far. It is a well-established and generally useful practice within the BBC to submit both television and radio programmes to post facto peer review. But programmes are not produced primarily to win the approbation of other broadcasters, gratifying though that will be to any producer. If I were myself responsible for the output, I would be undismayed to learn that in a general way one or two individual Governors had not much enjoyed a particular programme. The musical policy of Radio 1, for example, may not be geared to titillate the musical palate of a sexagenarian retired bureaucrat. But if, on the other hand, virtually a whole Board – a group of people more heterogeneous than is sometimes supposed – were to express a view that a particular programme had been wholly at odds with publicity-proclaimed BBC aims and standards, I hope I would want to think seriously about that, without regarding constructive criticism as a direction by inference.

As far as the scrutiny of scripts or the previewing or the pre-listening of programmes is concerned, I have already made it clear that I believe far too much weight is attached to past situations of a distinctly rare and exceptional kind. I repeat that, since I have joined the Board, I have not seen or heard, or wanted to see or hear in advance of transmission any script or programme. I found it fascinating that, when the BBC's own *Panorama* programme decided to focus on the question of 'whither the Corporation?',

and I myself was interviewed for that programme, far more importance was attached to a hypothetical role of 'censorship' than
either past experience or present reality merited. But the BBC has
long operated on the sensible footing of 'reference up'. In certain
very clearly-defined cases the makers of programmes are
specifically required to refer matters to higher management.
Given that the Board of Governors are not something separate
from the Corporation, but that in a juridical sense they are the
Corporation, it would be difficult to argue that there are no hypothetical circumstances in which a matter might be referred to the
Board of Governors itself, where the issue in question is whether
or not transmission of a particular programme would be in the
public interest. It is, after all, to protect the public interest that the
Governors are there at all. But we are dealing here with instances
which will certainly be rare and may well be hypothetical. I am in
no doubt that in almost all cases the Governors would prefer to
leave the matter to management and review any decision post-
transmission.

What of the future? We have a wonderful tendency in Britain to
take the continuity of our institutions as given, and therefore to
confine our questioning to adapting the role of bodies existing
almost as natural phenomena. The stimulus of being a Board
member through the process of Charter Renewal was that nothing
could be taken for granted:- not a continuing commitment to public service broadcasting; not to its expression specifically through
the BBC; not to the institutional and funding arrangements which
have so far buttressed it; not to the role in its affairs played by a
Board of Governors.

The task, the mission is what matters. And here, I confess, we
have not always succeeded in our presentation in separating the
primary from the secondary, in untangling the central role and
mission of a public broadcasting corporation in modern Britain
from the immensely complex, necessary but daunting infrastructure required to support it, and too often expressed in the fash-
ionable jargon of management-consultancy-speak. Since I
emerged into the civilised light of the BBC from the dim corridors
of the bureaucracy, I need no persuading about the necessity in
the modern world for strategies, plans, performance measures,
accountability requirements and effective controls. Far be it from
the recently appointed Chairman of the Corporation's Audit
Committee to discount the importance of getting our sums to add

up! Now, my colleagues and I believe above everything else that there is an irresistible case for the maintenance in Britain of a strong and vigorous public service broadcasting organisation, for very wide-ranging cultural, artistic and social reasons. My choice of the words 'cultural' and 'artistic' does not indicate a preference for Himalayan elitism. There is nothing indecent about fun; if it comes unaccompanied by unacceptable baggage, it is one of the more wholesome experiences of life. In the days when music-hall and the saucy postcard were parts of the British experience, they neither competed with, nor derogated from, Shakespeare on the one hand or Turner on the other. But at least it could be said that they were native products, a part of the differentiating indigenous experience. It would, or course, be a counter-productive absurdity to exclude from our airwaves and television screens all contributions from America or Australia or elsewhere. But these should be leaven, not the paramount part of the lump. The BBC's stall as set out in its document *Extending Choice,* suggested that our distinctive roles should be:-

to ensure that issues of importance to the nation, irrespective of immediate popular commercial appeal, will be properly reported, debated and analysed;

to reflect the full and diverse range of culture and entertainment in modern British society;

to increase the insights, understanding and knowledge of its audience across the full range of its programming; and

to be, as the world's most trusted international source of news and information, culture and entertainment, one of the primary means of communication between Britain and other countries.[1]

Personally I would put a special emphasis on two objectives entirely compatible with these headline statements of mission. I believe that as a bi-media broadcasting organisation, with international, national, regional and local capabilities, we have a particular part to play in what I think of as 'articulating the nation'. As I move around the country at public meetings, I find a very strong conviction that the listener or viewer supports a three-way process, whereby the region or locality better understands itself, the region or locality better understands the nation and the wider world beyond it, and the nation and the wider world form a well-rounded view of the region or locality. The BBC is uniquely well-placed to meet all of these needs.

I also believe strongly that a desire to succeed overall has to embrace a willingness to fail occasionally. A creative, cultural medium without risk will be a stagnant pool. How often, when I sit at the opera or a concert and read my programme notes before the lights go down, do I read how a particular piece at its first performance, or even for years after its first performance, was received with derision. I have formed a very clear view of the conservatism (with a small c) of the audience and particularly the radio audience. There is a strong loyalty to well-established programmes and artists, and even to the time-table for seeing or hearing them. Yet we need a broadcasting organisation capable of both daring and patience. I do not suggest for one moment that these qualities are absent from the make-up of many distinguished programme-makers employed by our commercial competitors. But I do say that the need to maximise subscription income or advertising revenues can be a strong constraint on programmatic adventure over the course of time.

It is more important to have such a public service broadcasting organisation that it is to defend any particular pre-existing feature of it. Thus we defend the licence fee, not because we think any other source of revenue appalling in principle, but because no one has so far identified an alternative secure basis of core funding consistent with our essential independence and impartiality. When we came to the preparation of *Extending Choice*, the Board were informed by a massive amount of work carried out by Task Forces of the vigorous and able within the Corporation, one of which had been specifically concerned with questions of governance. A critical stage was reached at the annual conference of the Boards of Governors and Management in 1992. We did not come together on that occasion to compile a series of justifications for the structure, role and purposes of the existing Board of Governors, but rather to consider from first principles the role (if any) to be performed by a body of lay people within or without the structure of a public service broadcasting organisation facing new and unprecedented challenges, but clear about its central mission. So what were the options as we understood them? Let me put them in the form of a series of questions.

1. Could one entrust the conduct of the most powerful media organisation in the country, funded by viewers and listeners through a compulsory licence fee, solely to a professional Board of Management?

2. Would there be merit in a new-style BBC Board which, like so many other important organisations in both the public and private sectors, would combine the talents of full-time executives with those of part-time non-executives?

3. Would there be merit in a different form of detached supervisory board – the 'board across the street' or even 'the board across town', which might relate either to the oversight of the BBC alone or to other and wider responsibilities for public sector broadcasting or the whole of broadcasting or particular aspects of them?

4 In the absence of a move to a 'mixed board' or 'the board across the street', did the existing parameters of Charter, convention and patterns of business allow the Board of Governors to define its distinctive role, to play that role adequately and to avoid usurping the proper role of the Board of Management led by the Director General?

Issues such as these have of course also been occupying the minds of others concerned in one way of another with Charter Review. In its own Consultation Document of November 1992 the Government tabled amongst its questions to be answered:-

Should changes be made in the functions of the Governors and the BBC Board of Management?

Should there be a Public Service Broadcasting Council either to regulate the BBC or to promote, finance and regulate public service broadcasting by the BBC and other services?
The Consultation Document commented:

There are those who believe that the Governors have been drawn too closely into the management of the BBC. On the other hand, others think that the Governors and the Board of Management could be merged, with the Governors becoming 'non-executive directors'.

And the document went on:

> In the future, the Governors could be given a different and
> clearer remit. They would be responsible for the Corporation's
> strategic policies and for appointing the most senior staff, but
> not for its day-to-day management. The Governors could super-
> vise the BBC rather than manage it. Or the Board could become
> regulators, without responsibilities for the BBC's policy-making.
> They might have a role setting the targets for improved
> efficiency and for monitoring whether these targets have been
> met. Another possibility would be to give them special respon-
> sibilities for finding out the public's views on the BBC's services,
> for ensuring that BBC managers are responsive to those views,
> and that the BBC's programme obligations are met. It has been
> suggested that the Governors should be elected from audi-
> ences, particularly those who watch or listen regularly to the
> BBC's audiences, and parliament and the Government repre-
> senting the general public.[2]

The Consultation Document went on to canvass options for a
Public Service Broadcasting Council, either to regulate the BBC
or more generally to promote public service broadcasting and per-
haps to take over some of the functions now carried out by the
Broadcasting   Standards   Council   and   the   Broadcasting
Complaints Commission.

After the publication of the Consultation Document by the
Government and of *Extending Choice* by the BBC, other well-
informed voices have joined the debate. Within the British Film
Institute's informative series on Charter Review, Colin Shaw
edited a series of contributions on the theme of 'Rethinking
Governance and Accountability'.[4] I have always taken anything
produced by Colin with the greatest seriousness since, over 40
years ago at University, he was an excellent producer of my very
bad acting, and I have thought a great deal about his suggestion –
not made for the first time in his own contribution to the booklet
– that the title of Governor should be replaced by the more precise title of Trustee. It is to be noted that in the section of *Extending
Choice* dealing with 'Direct Accountability', the side-heading to a
critical passage about the role of Governors is 'The Governors
have to act as trustees for the public interest', and this is developed
in the detailed text in the following words: '. . . the Board of

Governors must be – and be seen to be – a body competent to assure the independence, integrity and performance standards of the BBC as a public corporation seeking to identify and meet programme needs of viewers and listeners'.

As was to be expected, the role of the Governors was one of the matters touched upon by the National Heritage Select Committee in its consideration of the future of the BBC, leading in particular to a suggestion that before the appointment of future Governors there should be an extensive and public process of consultation, designed to produce a Board more representative than the present one, and with a provision for interview of a nominee by the Select Committee itself. The processes of appointment to this and other public bodies do indeed represent a fascinating and fruitful field for study and comment, but if I take you down this route we may begin to bear out the pietistic slogan painted on a barn wall in my native County Down: 'Time is short. Eternity where?'

Let me take you, though, through the thought processes of the Board itself as we discussed these important issues. It seemed to us inconceivable that the sole conduct of a major public service, consuming £1.5 billion annually of the public's money levied by licence fee, could be assigned to an executive board of professional managers alone. There must, in such a public service, be some means of representing and assuring the public interest. It may be said that the ruling philosophy in public management these days encourages devolution of many crucial and costly tasks to executive agencies under the charge of a management team headed by a Chief Executive. But such a team does not have *carte blanche*. It is for the responsible Secretary of State to approve a set of clear objectives for such an agent, accompanied by transparent measures of relevant performance. It really is not the case that, for example, Michael Bichard, as the Head of the Benefits Agency, is just given a third of our public revenues and told to get on with it. On the other hand, if this kind of strategic objective setting were to be left to Government in the case of a public broadcasting organisation such as the BBC, it would be difficult to argue that a body which often, and inevitably, presses upon sensitive points in the body politic was free of political pressure or implicit influence.

In this context I was amused to read in Paul Ferris's rather patchy life of Huw Wheldon, "Sir Huge", two versions of his view of what Governors should be doing. In the letter he actually sent to Charles Hill in July 1969, Wheldon argued that the Board 'must keep up the courage of the Corporation, keep it in bad times as well as good in the knowledge that what it presides over is a matter for pride and pleasure and not only for worry and anxiety'. Happily, there also survived among Wheldon's personal papers an earlier draft of the passage, which used faintly different language:

'Oh hell. What the bloody Board has to do is to keep its nerve (etc. etc.) To hell with them'.

You will not be too scandalised to hear that, now and then, a senior civil servant might well apostrophise his Ministerial bosses in not dissimilar terms, but we, in my old career, knew very well that Ministers could go many places where we could not go and would not go, and could effectively let us get on with our proper jobs by sheltering us from some, at least, of the political and public pressures now brought to bear upon any public service.

At first blush the idea of the 'mixed' Board had a certain attraction. After all, full-time executives and part-time non-executives work productively together on the boards of many corporate and other organisations. Such a model might well mean looking for directors with a very different profile and orientation than for most Governors under the existing system. Some previous knowledge of, and involvement in, broadcasting could be an advantage. But the BBC has to be regulated in the public interest as well as managed in its own interest. If a body of people were to have the deep involvement in the day-to-day running of the BBC inferred by the conflation of the Board of Governors with the Board of Management, it would be extremely difficult to argue that those same people could stand off, make, if necessary, critical as well as supportive judgements and avoid appearing to be totally 'captured' by the organisational machine. A corollary of a mixed board might well be the detachment of the regulatory role to be performed by a 'board across the street'. And here, frankly, we believe that it is necessary to steer a sensible course between excessive involvement and excessive detachment. If a body of people are to be in a position to guarantee to the public a broadcasting service of the necessary high standards, they need to be close enough to the organisation to make sound and realistic judgements about what is possible.

So we came to conclusion that the right model for the future relationship between Board of Governors and Board of Management would be loosely analogous with that between a Secretary of State with the central core of a Department on the

one hand and an executive agency on the other. This would mean
that the Governors would remain judicially responsible and ultimately accountable and would retain sufficiently close touch with
management to have an informed understanding of significant
issues; that they would define the broad role and mission of the
organisation and approve the strategic plans to fulfil it, with the
help of performance measures to inform their judgement; but
would draw a clear line between *governing* the BBC as ultimate
trustees for the public interest and *managing* it.

Thus it was that we came at last to those conclusions set out in
1993 in our published document *An Accountable BBC.* The government White paper, *The Future of the BBC*, published in July
1994,[4] made it clear that the work done in redefining responsibility had not been in vain. Noting that 'the governors were the
trustees of the national, or public, interest in broadcasting by the
BBC', it affirmed that their role was 'to look after the public's
interest in the BBC, not to manage it . . . to ensure that the BBC's
programmes, services and other activities reflect the needs and
interests of the public'. The governors also had responsibilities in
approving objectives, assessing performances, keeping in touch
with audiences and making sure that complaints are properly handled. They should also oversee the strategic direction of the BBC's
commercial activities. They must have a key responsibility for
financial oversight and a specified role in senior staff appointments.

If you ask the question 'Should the BBC be accountable, indeed
more accountable?', you are likely to receive the overwhelming
answer 'yes'. Public service and the requirement for accountability march closely together these days. But accountable to whom,
and in what way precisely? These are more complex questions to
answer. Since we live in a democracy, our elected Parliament must
have a significant role to play, and as we know, it is to Government
and Parliament we have to look for the renewal of a Charter, for
any desirable statutory regulation of broadcasting, for decisions
about the level of our licence fee, for approval of borrowing limits, and so on. I would suggest, though, that the political system of
the country does well to lead its public service broadcasting organisation on a very light rein. We will not be doing our duty, as an
independent, impartial and reliable source of news and current
affairs coverage, if we do not from time to time ruffle and irritate
the politicians of all parties. They in turn must have the right, as

do all our people, to criticise individual editorial or programme decisions if they think them wrong, but they do well, I would suggest, – as the great majority of them I believe do – to understand and if necessary defend our right to make them.

For us as Governors there will continue to be no greater responsibility than to defend robustly, and against all comers, the independence of the BBC. This does not mean signing up for the absurd adage 'the BBC right or wrong'. But it does mean resisting any form of pressure, direct or indirect, political or commercial, national or international. From time to time our legitimate activities will irritate or even infuriate individuals, institutions, foreign governments or states. When the BBC does so in the course of its proper duty, the Board of Governors must stand absolutely firm, and I assure you that we shall do so. We must of course recognise a form of accountability to our viewers and listeners, to those who pay the licence fee which is our main source of income. My strong view about that aspect of accountability is that we must be, in every sense and by a variety of means, accessible to viewers and listeners, and respectful of their views, as long as it is appreciated that a great cultural, artistic and news organisation cannot compose its schedules by referendum. Indeed, all talk of the 'audience' is something of a misnomer, because the BBC, of all broadcasting organisations, recognises a special duty to that complex of minorities which makes up the whole in a diverse society. Above all, though, that accountability which is at the heart of the role of Governors is, indeed, close to the concept of trusteeship as enunciated by Colin Shaw and others. We have to be the ultimate custodians, for the time being, of a great national treasure; a huge privilege and responsibility. We have now set out, more clearly I believe than ever before, how that responsibility should in our view be exercised. We identify three areas in which we must continue to exercise directly our ultimate authority over the BBC: appointment of the Director General and, with him, key senior executives; operation of a remuneration policy through a Governors' Remuneration Committee; and establishment of an Audit Committee along the lines envisaged by the Cadbury Report on Corporate Governance.

We accept, on the other hand, that in most matters – and in all the BBC's day-to-day affairs – authority is to be exercised by management on our behalf, and that our proper role as trustee is that of oversight. This entails in our view five distinct responsibilities:-

to stay closely in touch with public opinion;

to ensure that the BBC's overall strategy reflects the public's needs and interests;

to monitor and review performance against agreed objectives; to ensure compliance with statutory requirements and BBC guidelines; and

to guarantee regular reporting for the licence payer and to Parliament.

In much of what I have said I have been referring to the BBC as a whole. But it would be odd if what I have described as 'articulating the nation' did not involve a strong regional identity and presence. We have to reconcile the concept of 'one BBC', which in my view is part of our strength, with a real sensitivity to the separate needs, traditions and aspirations of discrete parts of the United Kingdom. It is for that purpose that what the Charter defines as the distinct broadcasting 'nations' of Scotland, Wales and Northern Ireland have been endowed with Broadcasting Councils concerned with the programme output specific to those countries. The BBC does not have subsidiary companies or a federal system analogous with Independent Television; nevertheless the Broadcasting Councils have, within their region, some of the characteristics of the Board of Governors at the centre. We have now moved to sharpen up the functions of these Councils by providing for them a standard role in receiving broadcasting plans and programme performance, seeking to stiffen the contacts with the communities they serve, and providing for each of them an opportunity for direct dialogue with the whole Board before we re-address wide strategy, priorities and plans at the hinge of each year. the government White Paper looks forward to a Charter redefinition of the role of the Broadcasting Councils which will sharpen up that role and clarify their responsibilities.

But above all I want, in conclusion, to say how proud I am to be a Governor of the BBC. We have been making our way through a prolonged and trying period of public scrutiny and internal re-organisation. We have had to support the management – and have gladly supported them – in measures never likely to gain easy or early popularity, but vitally necessary to enable the BBC to deliver the services we all want, to the standards we all want, within the resources likely to be available to it. Because it is the Governors I have been concerned with here, I have said relatively little about the Board of Management. But it is the obvious corollary of the re-definition of the Governors' role that a strong Board of Management should run the day-to-day affairs of the Corporation with the utmost efficiency and effectiveness, while never losing sight of our role and mission. I am confident that we have today a strong Board of Management, composed of highly talented people and dedicated to that task.

To a child of the 1930's , such as I was, the voice of the BBC was in one's ear almost as insistently as the voice of mother or teacher. In matters of the mind and spirit the BBC was, indeed, in a very real sense, mother and teacher to many of us. I have been glad to have the opportunity to pay back some small part of the debt I owe it.

NOTES

1. BBC, *Extending Choice: The BBC's Role in the New Broadcasting Age* (London: BBC, 1992).
2. Department of National Heritage, *The Future of the BBC: A Consultation Document*, Cm. 2098 (London: HMSO, 1992).
3. Colin Shaw (ed.), *Rethinking Governance and Accountability* (London: BFI, 1993).
4. Department of National Heritage, *The Future of the BBC: Serving the Nation, Competing World-wide*, Cm. 2621(London: HMSO, 1994).

*   This chapter is based on a talk originally given at a University of London seminar and was completed before the publication of the draft Charter of Agreement in the Broadcasting Bill.

SERVING THE NATION: COMPETING WORLD-WIDE

Bob Phillis

I should like to begin by explaining the title because it certainly isn't mine. In fact, it's Her Majesty's Government's , which published a White Paper on 7 July 1994 called *The Future of the BBC, Serving the Nation, Competing World-wide*[1] the implications of which I will try to outline here. But what I'll be doing is addressing, not so much the particularities of Northern Ireland, but putting that in the context of the future of broadcasting in general and the way we see the role for the BBC within that.

But, of course, like everybody else, I share the high hopes that the peace process will come to its ultimate and successful conclusion and that it will succeed not only for everybody that lives in Northern Ireland, but because the prospects and reality of peace will certainly shift the preoccupations which, very properly, have been the broadcasters' for the last twenty-five years or so. It will affect us as broadcasters because we no longer concentrate quite so much of our energy and our time, whether in News and Current Affairs or indeed in Drama, on the problems that the people of Northern Ireland have all had to live with.

I also believe that the BBC can, as a public service broadcaster, play a crucial role at this time – not simply in recording the reality and the process of peace itself, but also helping to explain, to equip, to inform people in the future. And we are going to be able to focus on a whole range of different things that maybe we've been a little restricted in covering in the past. First of all we will be concentrating on the needs of the communities themselves, providing that platform for open debate where all of the issues can be discussed and be debated in perhaps a much easier forum than has been possible in the past. And, of course, it is our role on radio and on television, to reflect all of the diverse leisure interests, the rich music, the literature, the drama, the sporting heritage, which makes up the background to Northern Ireland and the peoples within it. I hope that we are going to have more opportunity as broadcasters to portray Northern Ireland, both at home in Britain and abroad, in a way that reflects the warmth, the dynamism, the humour, the energy, the creativity of everybody that lives there, and the spectacular beauty of the country which I've had the privilege of visiting many, many times since I visited in 1968.

Elsewhere in this volume, Pat Loughrey discusses what has been achieved, even during the difficult, troubled period, in reflecting the diversity of at least some of those needs. And I would like to add my thanks, congratulations and appreciation to all of those who have worked in broadcasting and the media – whether in television, radio, press; whether in the BBC or our commercial competitors – for what has been achieved. Because I think, particularly in the field of News and Current Affairs, that that skill, that insight, that sensitivity in reporting, and very often the courage to grapple with such difficult issues, is something which distinguishes a long stream of journalists and broadcasters who have worked in Northern Ireland over the last 25 years, and I believe we owe a very deep vote of thanks. And I include, of course, current people in the field.

During 1994, the BBC celebrated seventy years of broadcasting in Northern Ireland. And the BBC is pretty good at celebrating things. We do a lot of it. We mark events, we congratulate ourselves for the prizes we win, and we find opportunities to honour particular occasions. There's been a bit of that over the last few years, with the commemorations of D-Day and Arnhem. And in 1995, on Radio 3, the whole year was dedicated to 'A Year of British Music and Culture'. It should, of course, more correctly have been described as 'The Year of United Kingdom Music and Culture', as it did indeed involve contributions from Northern Ireland as well. We also marked and celebrated the fiftieth anniversary of the end of the Second World War during this year as well. And I mention it because, for those of interested in the history of broadcasting and the reporting of conflict, it's very interesting indeed to look back to the events of 1944. (I can categorically refute any suggestion that CNN must have been on the beaches of Normandy. If they had been, they would no doubt have been using carrier pigeons to get the messages back.) Actually it was the BBC which was at the cutting edge of technology then, when we had shellac recording disks which were brought back across the channel to relay, for the first time in war reporting, accounts of events within hours of them happening. The first ever live reporting of a wartime situation followed the D-Day landings, about 18 days later, when the BBC was able to transmit direct from the Normandy bridgeheads back into the BBC in London. This was way ahead of the Americans. For those who are interested in that aspect of broadcasting history, it's instructive to compare the broadcast coverage of the Falklands and the Gulf War and other recent conflicts. There are some interesting parallels and contrasts with the difficulties that there have been in reporting on the troubles here in Northern Ireland.

But returning to less serious matters, in 1996 we will be celebrating 60 years of BBC television, and that very conveniently coincides with the end of our existing Charter as a public service broadcaster. And that's really my link into the future. I want to try to talk just a little about how the changing circumstances in Northern Ireland might fit into the changing broadcasting and media world of tomorrow and I come back to the Government's White Paper.

I have to say that, when I joined the BBC, I didn't expect the outcome that seems to have been secured. There is no doubt that the tide running in the government of the day was an active consideration of breaking up the BBC or privatising the BBC, or requiring the BBC to carry advertising. And had that happened, then the whole shape of public service broadcasting in Britain would have changed forever. And one only needs to look at events in Canada, in Germany and in New Zealand, where their public service broadcasters have been made 'a little bit pregnant' with advertising revenue, and you see how much of the rich diversity of programmes that we try to make and schedule, as a public service broadcaster, gets driven from the schedules altogether. And I don't over-exaggerate the situation or the risk to both the scale and funding of the organisation. As it happens, the only part of the BBC which is at risk of privatisation, is the transmission operation which is currently the subject of a review.

So, although we won the battle against having to carry advertising as a source of funding for the BBC, we nevertheless had to address the changes that the future is going to bring to the industry of which we are a part. Because there was another school of thought, and a school of thought which surprisingly was espoused by my friend and colleague Melvyn Bragg for a while, that the BBC should only concern itself with the 'Himalayan Heights' – that we should only provide that type of programming that other broadcasters would not make. Once again, if you define the role of a public service broadcaster and the BBC in that way, then you diminish that rich variety of programmes that the White Paper has confirmed as an essential part of our remit. It has, I am pleased to say, reaffirmed our role as a public service broadcaster that has to make programmes in radio and in television, serving all interests, all ages, all cultures – and to schedule them at times when people are there to view them or listen to them. And that's something which I take a great deal of satisfaction from. Specifically, the White Paper charges us with sustaining the two television networks nationally, the five national radio networks, the national radio systems in Northern Ireland, in Wales and Scotland, and the many local radio stations throughout England itself. And they will continue to be funded by the licence fee.

The White Paper also, very properly, emphasises the need for the BBC to reflect to the nation as a whole, much more of that rich diversity of culture that there is throughout the entire United Kingdom. And I have to say that there's no doubt that, in the past, the BBC has been too centred upon the metropolitan and the South East area of England. The White Paper tells us to address that issue and we will; we already are. We've made a firm commitment that, over the next three years, we will divert £75m worth of programme-making expenditure from London and the South East to the nations and to the regions around the country. And there is a firm commitment to ensuring that all parts of the United Kingdom have their programmes and their cultures and their backgrounds more adequately reflected on the BBC networks as a whole. And if you want evidence of the progress that Pat Loughrey and his colleagues are making in Northern Ireland, I can tell you that in the space of only a little over two years, the number of hours of programming now seen on the network as a whole has shifted from 3 to 30 hours a year, and that is to be built upon and increased still further. And in that same period, drama from Northern Ireland for the network has increased from 2 to 10 hours a year. And drama is our most expensive and one of our most important genres of television programming. This is a very real commitment to Northern Ireland which we will sustain.

But there are those who think that the argument about the future of the BBC is over, and that the White Paper has ensured a licence fee funded BBC for ten years to the year 2006. It isn't as easy as that. Firstly, although the Government has reaffirmed its intention to fund us by the licence fee, it hasn't told us how it's going to assess or calculate the licence fee, beyond 1996. There is also a provision that the whole concept of licence fee funding is going to be re-examined in the year 2001. I think that we will sustain the principle of licence fee funding, but we are going to have to fight hard to maintain the level of that funding, necessary to sustain the programme services that we envisage during the next decade. And the reason for that is that over the next 10 years I believe that, whether we like it or not, there's going to be much more competition for people's viewing and listening time, and there's going to be much more pressure on the absolute level of the licence fee and whether or not it keeps pace with the Retail Price Index.

And so it seems clear to me that the BBC does not have any option but to accept change. We cannot simply stick our head in the sand and say we don't like this multi-media, multi-channel competitive world; we're not just simply going to maintain our chasteness as a public service broadcaster and argue the case for adequate licence fee funding. To do that would be to ignore the reality of this technological future that we are being thrust into. And let me just put the process of change into historical context because of course, our origins were as a broadcasting monopoly in radio. We had a broadcasting monopoly in television until ITV got underway. And when ITV came on to the scene, there was that almost accidental separation of the funding, between commercial television and the BBC itself. We compete for audiences, but ITV was to be funded by advertising sales, whereas the BBC remained funded by the licence fee. And when Channel Four came along in 1982 (one of the great innovations in British broadcasting) it, too, was funded indirectly by advertising, but operated within a very particular remit. But this simple division of funding is now changing very rapidly. And it's changing because of the technologies of cable, of fibre optics, of satellite and of the digital age around the UK. BSkyB seems to have made an enormous recovery from its difficult start, if the price at which it was floated on the stock market was any indication. Subscription revenues are going to be an increasingly important way in which broadcasting is financed in Britain.

But, in addition to competition for our viewing and listening time, there is also going to be competition for rights in all sorts of programmes; there's going to be competition for talent (and talent is a very scarce commodity) whether that is writing talent or technical and design skills. There is going to be tremendous demand and some of these large international players believe that they can buy audiences for new services by buying rights to sporting events, to programmes or individuals on screen to present and to perform.

And these new services will affect viewing and listening patterns in Britain. Our average viewer in Britain today watches about four hours of television a day, with BBC and ITV roughly equal during peak time and satellite and cable taking three per cent of the audience in peak time. Across the day ITV and Channel Four have a slight advantage on BBC1 and BBC2 taken together and cable and satellite viewing is six per cent of the total. Some of the estimates that we see predict that within 10 years almost fifty per cent of homes in Britain will have cable and/or satellite, providing alternative viewing and listening opportunities. Although I cannot offer an explanation it is, perhaps, interesting to note that the rate of penetration of satellite and cable here in Northern Ireland is about half that in the rest of the UK. My colleagues tell me that we are still seeing predictions of some 300,000 homes cabled or receiving satellite here within five years. This is going to change again the way people use their television sets.

These changes will be driven further by the technologies of convergence – the convergence between broadcasting and telecommunications and computers, and the power of digital technology. There is much talk about the Digital Superhighways, although there is also a huge amount of 'superhypeways' about what services will actually be delivered, and by whom, and at what cost to the individual. I have some healthy scepticism about the scale, scope, timing and potential of digital superhighways because, even if the technologists are able to give us the 150 or the 500 channel home, what they cannot provide in such volume is the quality and range of programming that people will want to watch – and to pay for. But having said that, the technological revolution is going to happen. Fibre optics and digital compression does already give the possibility of 500 channels and there are cities in the United States already being cabled or linked by satellite to receive it.

In terms of potential demand for new services, some of the research we've done in Britain suggests that, for the moment, most British homes would like to see more than the four channels currently available free, but most of them say that, if they could choose to meet their own particular viewing habits, somewhere between six and ten is the number of channels they feel would satisfy their needs. There is an obverse reaction from many households who say that they don't want 30, 40, 50, 60 channels, where too much time is spent zapping through to find something that's interesting. Such people are indicating that they would rather have a more limited number of quality channels to view. But such reactions are not going to stop the technologists driving forward.

But multi-channel homes, provided by digital compression on satellite, or digital compression terrestrially, is not the only new technology. A huge amount of money is being spent by British Telecom on video-on-demand, intending to use copper wire, telephone cables and even fibre optic cables to enable the viewer to dial up programming of their choice on the telephone. The BBC and others are participating with BT in order to try to understand whether this vision can become a reality, whether it can be made to work and what consumer interest there might be in such a service. Trials that have taken place in East Anglia recently suggest that it is technologically possible. And the capacity of the file servers that BT has in mind are immense; they can store millions of different programmes which any one of us could, in theory, link up to on our telephone line and be able to view on the television screen on demand – that is to say at a time of our own choosing.

Apple Computers and ICL are developing monitors or PCs on which you can watch television programmes, and with which potentially you can interact. And I think it will be very interesting to see how the television screen that we're used to seeing our programmes on now might be supplemented or replaced by people being able to tap in and watch television programming on their own computer. For this reason, the BBC is actively exploring and developing new inter-active services from CD-ROM to the Networking Club on the Internet.

All of these developments are inevitably going to mean greater competition for viewers' time and a fragmenting of the audience. And, in addition, we also have to take account of the other new services that the technologists tell us will be available – home shopping, home banking, home booking of your travel requirements, the electronic newspaper, piped down the line onto your television screen, and educational services galore. So, inevitably, there is going to be pressure on the amount of viewing time that we spend on our terrestrial broadcast channels: ITV, Channel Four, BBC1, BBC2 and Channel Five – if it actually happens.

And what will be the impact of these changes? I have already indicated that I don't think that there will be anywhere near enough programming to sustain this massive array of choice, and many of these services will inevitably have to rely on more and more cheap, imported, recycled programming, much of it coming from the United States, because the United States is the biggest production market in the world. It is true that the consumer is going to have much more choice in self-scheduling. I use the word consumer deliberately. I personally much prefer the word audience, but it will be consumers who will buy these different services and build their own schedule during the day providing, of course, that they perceive that they are getting value for the money spent.

What we don't know is what price they're going to be prepared to pay for such 'choice' – and indeed all of those involved in this particular game are equally unclear. But the reason that I'm emphasising the point is that it seems to me the BBC is going to be under pressure in sustaining a universal licence fee at our current level of real total income. And as we move through this next decade, the real value of total licence fee income, currently £1.6 billion a year to the BBC, is likely to decline. So what does the BBC do? Do we stick our heads in the sand and say, we have to live with it, and scale down our services as a result, or do we look for the opportunity to make our programme assets work harder to earn income to put back into programme making for the benefit of domestic audiences? That, very simply, is the approach that we've decided to follow.

But there are also opportunities and challenges to an organisation like the BBC. We are the largest maker of programmes in the world outside the United States and on a par with Japan. We have the largest library and archive in the world, over a quarter of a million different programmes stretching back over 40 years, and there will be demands from people who are interested in niche programming, in particular types of programming. And this gives the BBC an opportunity to use our programme assets.

In addition to our libraries and archives, the BBC is the largest news gathering organisation in the world. When you put together our strengths in local, regional, national and in international news gathering for both television and radio, we actually do have a huge resource in terms of the news services that we can provide. And I also want to emphasise the importance to the BBC of education programmes and services – not simply programmes made for schools, colleges and universities – but the whole panoply of education, enrichment and learning skills that we can provide, as a core requirement of a public service broadcaster. The Board of Governors and the Board of Management place a very high priority on this role, not only nationally but internationally; not only in broadcast terms, but in interactive and CD-ROM terms as well, providing wider access to the programmes we make for our core services.

So that's why the title of the White Paper, Serving the Nation, (our prime public service purpose) and Competing World-wide is so important. Because whilst all these technologies are clearly a challenge and a threat, they do also provide an opportunity. At the BBC we recognise that our first and foremost purpose is to make programmes for the United Kingdom, but if we also take the opportunity of making those programme assets (the intellectual property in our programming) work harder to generate more income internationally, we can supplement the licence fee to help fund the programmes we wish to make, and to compensate any shortfall that may result from pressure on the licence fee.

This is not an easy task. We have had to organise ourselves to do it. We have brought all of our international operations in radio and television, public service or commercial, together under BBC Worldwide, and we are certainly looking to make our programming more widely available on an international basis, not simply through selling our programmes but through offering BBC television channels internationally, to complement the strength of World Service Radio. So we have a BBC 24 hour news and information channel, which you can see in much of the Far East, the Subcontinent and now in Japan (with a Japanese translation), in the Middle East (in Arabic), and from January 1995, in Europe with a 24 hour BBC news and information service and a BBC entertainment service, respectively called BBC World and BBC Prime.

But there is something I want to emphasise. The BBC is not diverting any licence fee income to finance our commercial operations. With the exception of making news programmes to an international news agenda, these services are acquiring the rights in programmes that we make for our UK audiences and presenting and packaging them to a wider audience internationally in order to generate new revenues for the BBC. And, in addition to the possibility of an international entertainment channel, in each and every case addressed to the particular market we're broadcasting to, there is the chance to offer blocks of documentary, natural history, education or children's programming, carrying the BBC brand and reputation to a wider international market place. If successful, this will help to sustain the services that we are obliged to provide as the prime and fundamental purpose of a public service broadcaster in the United Kingdom.

This can only be achieved by working with partners around the world, but we will always insist that the BBC has editorial control over any BBC-branded services. And, sometimes, that editorial control and the values that we strive to sustain in our news coverage result in difficulties. We broadcast a 24 hour news and information service called World Service Television as part of the Star TV satellite service to China. Shortly after acquiring Star TV some two years ago, Rupert Murdoch made a very profound declaration to the world, outlining an ambition for his organisation, News Corporation, to surround the world with international news services from which no totalitarian regime in the world would be able to escape. Well, unfortunately, the Beijing government didn't quite see it that way and Rupert Murdoch was faced with a very clear option. Whether to veto, censor or discard the BBC World News, because of its uncomfortable tendency to talk about Tiannamen Square, Hong Kong, Chairman Mao's sex life and other abuses of human rights, or jeopardise the wide commercial and broadcasting ambitions in China? And Mr Murdoch made his choice. The BBC World News service is no longer broadcast into China because we would not accept or allow anyone to censor the editorial values and structure of a BBC news service to any part of the world. So there are hard choices. But it's taking us back to that public service core and our public service values which means we have to eschew commercial considerations if it is at the cost of our editorial and programming values.

We have clearly been set a challenge in the White Paper to 'Serve the Nation and to Compete World-wide'. But we have to succeed because, if we don't succeed in bridging that gap we can see coming in our financing, then a government at some future time is going to conclude that the BBC should be advertiser funded. And if the BBC were financed by advertising, you would not see the same scheduling and you would not see the same range of programming that we actually aspire to try to deliver today.

I would like to conclude by talking about the Irish dimension in what I've been saying internationally. I have said that we need to portray the diversity and the richness of the differences of our cultures within the UK, but that must also apply in what we try to do internationally. And it seems to me that there's a massive audience internationally that would certainly be interested in the affairs and the culture of Northern Ireland and Ireland more widely. And it seems to me we have to look for the opportunities of bringing some of the programming that is made in Northern Ireland to wider audiences overseas. And the sort of strategy that I have been trying to sketch out does give us that opportunity. And it's one that I personally welcome.

I would like to finish by saying that I do believe that the future of the BBC in Northern Ireland is in very good hands with its current Governor, its current Controller and their particular team. No part of the BBC is ever worried or concerned by constructive criticism, because it's through constructive criticism and debate that we can set ourselves higher standards in attempting to serve our audiences more effectively. And that applies every bit as much in Northern Ireland as it does to anywhere else in the UK.

NOTES

1. Department of National Heritage, *The Future of the BBC: Serving the Nation, Competing World-wide*, Cm. 2621 (London: HMSO, 1994).

NOTES ON CONTRIBUTORS

MARTIN McLOONE is Senior Lecturer in Media Studies and Head of School, Media and Performing Arts at the University of Ulster.

PADDY SCANNELL is Senior Lecturer in Media Studies at the University of Westminster.

DES CRANSTON is Senior Lecturer in Media Studies at the University of Ulster.

JAMES HAWTHORNE is a former Controller BBC NI. He is currently Visiting Professor of Media Studies at the University of Ulster.

PAT LOUGHREY is currently Controller BBC NI.

KEITH KYLE is a former journalist with the BBC and is currently Visiting Lecturer in History at the University of Ulster.

KEITH BAKER is a former Head of News and Current Affairs and is currently Chief Editorial Advisor at the BBC NI.

DAVID BUTLER is Lecturer in Media Studies at the University of Ulster.

LIZ FAWCETT is a former journalist with BBC NI and is currently Lecturer in Media Studies at the University of Ulster.

KEN BLOOMFIELD is currently National Governor of the BBC for Northern Ireland.

BOB PHILLIS is Deputy Director-General of the BBC.